P9-CFD-709

Better Homes and Gardens®

CLUTTER CUTTERS

STORE IT WITH STYLE

Meredith® Books

Des Moines, Iowa

Clutter Cutters: Store It with Style
Editor: Vicki Leigh Ingham
Contributing Field Editors: Susan Andrews, Miranda Hitt, Donna Talley
Senior Associate Design Director: Doug Samuelson
Contributing Graphic Designer: Craig Hanken, Studio p2
Copy Chief: Terri Fredrickson
Publishing Operations Manager: Karen Schirm
Edit and Design Production Coordinator: Mary Lee Gavin
Book Production Managers: Pam Kvitne, Marjorie J. Schenkelberg, Rick von Holdt, Mark Weaver
Contributing Copy Editor: Stacey Shildroth
Contributing Proofreaders: David Krause, Beth Lastine, Nancy Ruhling
Contributing Photographers: Tria Giovan, Bob Greenspan, Deborah Whitlaw Llewellyn, Michael Partenio, Jay Wilde
Contributing Photo Stylist: Rebecca Jerdee
Indexer: Sharon Duffy
Editorial Assistant: Kaye Chabot

Meredith® Books
Editor in Chief: Linda Raglan Cunningham
Design Director: Matt Strelecki
Managing Editor: Gregory H. Kayko
Executive Editor: Denise L. Caringer

Publisher: James D. Blume
Executive Director, Marketing: Jeffrey Myers
Executive Director, New Business Development: Todd M. Davis
Executive Director, Sales: Ken Zagor
Director, Operations: George A. Susral
Director, Production: Douglas M. Johnston
Business Director: Jim Leonard

Vice President and General Manager: Douglas J. Guendel

Better Homes and Gardens® **Magazine**
Editor in Chief: Karol DeWulf Nickell
Deputy Editor, Home Design: Oma Blaise Ford

Meredith Publishing Group
President, Publishing Group: Stephen M. Lacy
Vice President-Publishing Director: Bob Mate

Meredith Corporation
Chairman and Chief Executive Officer: William T. Kerr

In Memoriam: E. T. Meredith III (1933-2003)

Copyright © 2004 by Meredith Corporation, Des Moines, Iowa. First Edition.
All rights reserved. Printed in the United States of America.
Library of Congress Control Number: 2004102155
ISBN: 0-696-22128-4

All of us at Meredith® Books are dedicated to providing you with information and ideas to enhance your home. We welcome your comments and suggestions. Write to us at: Meredith Books, Home Decorating and Design Editorial Department, 1716 Locust St., Des Moines, IA 50309-3023.
If you would like to purchase any of our home decorating and design, cooking, crafts, gardening, or home improvement books, check wherever quality books are sold. Or visit us at: bhgbooks.com

TABLE OF CONTENTS

A Space That Works

My crowded home office (**opposite**) housed a computer desk, a window unit air-conditioner, an uncomfortable space-eating bench, painting supplies, paintings, and a tall bookcase. A dining room chair made a miserable desk chair. The solution? Move out the bench, buy an office chair, and make a worktable from two file cabinets and plywood. To hide the air-conditioner and more, I built a table from plywood and skirted it. Boxes and baskets hold painting and stationery supplies.

BEFORE

CONFESSIONS OF A CLUTTERER

BY VICKI INGHAM

It's so easy to accumulate clutter. Believe me, I know. I saved old magazines and interesting articles for at least a decade, thinking I would get around to reading them. I couldn't throw away letters, birthday cards, and holiday cards because I felt as if I would be

discarding the relationships they represent. I was afraid to toss cancelled checks, so they filled the attic.

Most of my chaos is out there for everyone to see. Some people, however, hide their clutter-prone ways by stuffing everything into closets and cabinets. The house looks tidy to casual visitors, but trouble lurks behind those closed doors. In both cases, the energy wasted searching for a missing shoe or misplaced airline tickets is reason enough to begin decluttering and get organized.

This process may require behavioral modification—learning to let go of things you don't use, don't need, or

don't really like. Getting rid of clutter is also a matter of changing family habits, making decisions about what to keep and where to put it instead of letting things pile up wherever you happen to drop them.

The payoffs, however, are worth the effort: Piles of papers and closets full of junk represent decisions deferred; they become a burden weighing you down. When you begin making decisions (keep, toss, give away, or store), you reassert control over the clutter and over your life.

And that's only half the story: Organizing and storing the stuff that remains is the other half. This book shows a variety of storage solutions, from custom-designed,

Too Much Stuff

I moved most of the photo albums (above) to a hall closet, freeing shelf space for baskets that now hold paper and office supplies (opposite). Moving books to the edge of the shelf creates a clean, united front. Matching boxes of various sizes hold stationery, props, and photos for painting. The skirted table makes a pleasing focal point and hides the window unit air-conditioner and painting supplies.

custom-built dream closets and cupboards to clever combinations of repurposed or ready-made items designed to store your stuff with style. You also will find suggestions from expert organizers for systems to help you stay clutter-free.

Peace at Last

Following the advice of Kellie Kramer, an organizing consultant, I began tackling my chaotic office by moving the black bench into another room. The rolls of paper and canvas stacked in the corner moved to a closet, liberating space to tuck paintings there. I also moved the bookcase out of the corner, pulling it toward the center

of the side wall. Being able to see into the corner makes the space feel larger and lighter.

The air-conditioner in its box has to be stored in this room, but it moved to the spot formerly occupied by the bench. In its place I brought in a pair of two-drawer file cabinets and laid a 24×40-inch plywood panel over them. (I painted the plywood to match the cabinets.) This provided much-needed work space beside the computer and a spot for the printer. Now all of my papers are in these two cabinets. To keep my "action" files out where I can see them, a clear acrylic stepped organizer sits beside the printer. It holds folders for bills, receipts, catalog orders, and vacation plans.

To make space for office supplies, I cleared some of the bookshelves of photo albums. Baskets hold paper, envelopes, pens, and paper clips. To hide the air-conditioner and provide a restful focal point for the room, I built a three-sided table and covered it with a no-sew skirt.

Now my office is a clean, serene, and orderly space. I love it!

Table and No-Sew Skirt

Have a home improvement center cut a 4×8-foot sheet of ¾-inch plywood in half lengthwise; then cut one half into two 28-inch pieces and the other half into two 40-inch pieces. Use 3-inch angle brackets to attach the two 24×28-inch pieces (the sides) to one 24×40-inch panel (the top). Screw the remaining 24×40-inch piece to the back, aligning the top edges and sides.

To skirt the table, cover the top with a thin sheet of batting, stapling it to the edges of the plywood. From the fabric cut a top panel, adding 1 inch all around, and staple it over the batting. Cut side panels, adding 1 to 2 inches for hems at the top and bottom edges. Fuse the bottom hem with fusible adhesive tape. Fold the top hem and staple it to the plywood. Wrap the front edge of the panel around the plywood leg and staple it in place. For the skirt front, add 6 to 8 inches to the width to allow for corner pleats. Staple in place. Hot glue braiding over the staples.

ENTRIES

Does your entry welcome you home or make you want to turn and run? The entrance used most often—whether it's the front door, back door, or access through the garage—can easily become a dumping ground for dropping off things on your way into or out of the house. With some organizational help and creative storage, however, you can make this area an attractive, functional, and efficient transitional space.

According to *feng shui* practitioners, a cluttered entry blocks the flow of energy into the house and is an obstacle to your emotional well-being. Whether you subscribe to this ancient Chinese design philosophy or not, it's certainly true that an entry littered with coats, boots, and stacks of mail can send a "do not enter" signal to friends and visitors. The piles of stuff also can make it physically difficult to get into the house.

Here's how to begin breaking down the obstacle course created by clutter.

First analyze the space. Ask yourself: What doesn't belong there? What could be stashed somewhere else? What needs to stay?

What do you do as you go out the door or as you come in? Take off a coat and shoes or boots? Prop an umbrella to dry? Set down your purse or briefcase and keys? Is this where the kids drop their backpacks, books, and sporting gear when they come in? Is this where the dog leash needs to hang?

Start by clearing everything out of the entry so you have a clean slate. Then assess which kinds of furnishings or accessories will address your coming-and-going needs. Consider providing a landing pad for your keys, purse, briefcase, library books, and grocery list—anything you want to take with you when you leave the house. If family members come and go at different hours, consider hanging a blackboard beside the door to write messages, notes, and reminders.

If you drop the mail at this spot when you come in, don't let it stack up there. Immediately sort bills and move them to your office or bill-paying area; toss the junk mail in the recycling bin. Put magazines and catalogs where you're likely to read them (and if you haven't looked at them a month later, throw them away or recycle them).

Entry Gallery

Turn the hall into a fanciful coat closet with decorative hooks attached to the wall at different levels according to the heights of family members. Identify the owner of each hook with a framed snapshot. Include a hook for Fido's leash. A portable chest with color-coded wicker drawers gives each person a place for gloves, hats, and scarves.

- -

➤➤READER TIP

When we moved into a new house in 1983, I bought some vinyl-coated wire baskets in a metal frame and put it in a closet just inside the door from the garage. Each family member has a basket. Every day I put mail or odds and ends in the appropriate basket. It is a great way to keep kitchen counters clear of gloves, sunglasses, magazines, or baseball hats. (There is also a basket for batteries.) My two grown sons still check their baskets when they come over to see what I've saved for them—an article I saw in the paper about a friend, a second set of photos of my cute grandchildren, or mail that occasionally comes in their names. The best part is that I can take care of sorting right away and don't have to remember to give things to them when they come over.

Linda Dieleman
Plymouth, Minnesota

Thinking Inside the Box

A chest or paired stacks of wooden drawers offer a tidy way to organize the paraphernalia that collects inside the entry. Use the drawers to stash items you need as you go out—gloves, hats, scarves, dog leashes, games to keep kids occupied in the car—and keep a basket or tray on top for keys. A wall-mounted rack receives newspapers, magazines, and mail. This is a good place to have a lamp on a timer with a low-wattage bulb to light the entry when you come home after dark.

Space for a Mudroom

Create a mudroom off the back entry or inside the garage with a custom-built wall of open storage (opposite). For each family member, there's a place to hang coats and an umbrella, overhead space for sports equipment, and a drawer for necessities. The 11-year-old daughter, for example, uses her drawer (above) to keep her jump rope, hat, and school projects handy. Raising the drawers off the floor provides room for muddy boots underneath and makes a convenient bench to sit on.

- -

▶▶READER TIP

One of my favorite ways to control clutter is to use the shoe bags that hang on the back of the door. Instead of using the overdoor hangers that come with the bag, I screw cup hooks into the door to support the bag. I have one on the back of my coat closet door to hold gloves, umbrellas, outdoor seasonal flags, ice scraper for the car, and so on. I use one right inside the garage for gardening tools and one in the laundry/utility room for extension cords, vacuum attachments, polishing rags, and other cleaning supplies.

Teresa Phillips
Goshen, Ohio

Built-Ins and Options

A wall of custom-designed cubbies at the back or side door (above) can store cleaning supplies, tools, picnic gear, and sporting equipment as well as coats and shoes. If the front door is your main entry for family and guests, a piece of furniture, such as an antique tansu chest (opposite), offers space for outerwear, backpacks, sweaters, and even shoes.

A Place for Everything

A well-planned wall of open shelves, cupboards, and coat pegs (opposite) tames chaos at the back door. Baskets collect sports gear, cleaning supplies, and recycling items. Boots tuck neatly under the bench. Even in a tiny space (above), a movable cart with baskets can serve as a collecting point.

▶▶READER TIP

My husband owns a huge collection of baseball caps. They took over the hall closet until I found ready-to-assemble shoe holders. They are square with inserts dividing the box into smaller squares. I purchased several and put them on the top shelf in my hall closet and they work wonderfully for storing his baseball hats as well as mittens and gloves. I can put two or three items in each small cubby.

Pat Perkins
Verona, Wisconsin

Storage Bins

Tuck a wire basket under a bench (below) for display or to collect newspapers and magazines for recycling. Install wall-hung shelves to place everything at the right height (opposite): mittens and homework are at a child's level; keys, mail, and decorative objects are at adult eye level. Label the metal bins (right) so everyone knows where items belong. An old chest beside the door (below right) catches backpacks so they don't end up on the kitchen counter.

>>**READER TIP**

One way I eliminate junk mail during the winter is to toss it into a basket near the fireplace and use it for kindling. It's a great way to keep a fire going and get rid of junk mail so it doesn't get into the wrong hands.

Kari Greer
Florence, South Carolina

Hang Ups

Peg racks are perfect for hanging up muddy shoes or coats. To make one like this (above), start with ³/₄-inch dowels and a 1×4 board long enough to fit your wall. Drill a hole slightly smaller than the dowel halfway through the board. Glue the dowel into the hole and secure it with a screw driven in from the back of the board. Space two dowels 4 inches apart for a pair of shoes. You also can use cabinet pulls or doorknobs instead of pegs (opposite). Or shop flea markets for antique garden fencing and hang it on the wall upside down to make a coatrack (right).

FAMILY ROOMS

- -

Whether you call it a den, a family room, or a living room, this is the common space for gathering and relaxing. It's where you sink into a comfortable chair at the end of the day to watch television or read the paper. It's also likely to be the room where you gather with friends—and where, the afternoon before the party, you're frantically stuffing magazines into cupboards and toys into chests to give the look of welcoming order to the room. Here are some ideas for real decluttering.

What are the clutter villains in family rooms and living rooms? Stacks of newspapers and magazines sprout here like mushrooms; videos, toys, hobby projects, and pet toys likely crowd the floors, tabletops, and shelves; and you may even trip over shoes that didn't make it to the closet.

To tame the clutter in this room, begin by listing the activities that go on here. Reading, watching television, relaxing with friends? Is this where children play and pets nap? What really needs to be here to support those activities? Aside from training family members to put away shoes and jackets, much of your decluttering in this area involves providing storage that organizes your belongings into tidy stacks, hides it behind cabinet doors, or stashes it in attractive, accessible containers.

Start with surfaces: Place magazines and newspapers in a basket instead of letting them pile up on the floor or coffee table. If you haven't read the newspaper after a week, recycle it. If you like to keep magazines after you've read them, consider storing them in cardboard units that you can stack in a cabinet or on a bookshelf. Look for these organizers at office supply stores. Or go through the magazines and cut out the articles you want to keep, file these in labeled folders or photo albums, and throw the magazines away.

>>READER TIP

Instead of investing in containers all at once (which can be expensive), I bought one plastic container every time I went shopping. Before long I had enough to organize everything.

Tammy Goebel
Bridgeton, Missouri

Creative Side Tables

Use flea market finds for side tables that double as storage units. An old kitchen cupboard turned on its side (above) serves as a bookcase. Stacked suitcases (right and opposite) can store craft and hobby supplies, records you don't need to access often, old photo albums, or even out-of-season clothing. Neatly stacked matching suitcases create a visually unified, formal effect; mismatched cases are more casual.

Wraparound Storage

Shop home stores, discount stores, or storage supply shops for versatile cubes that can be stacked to embrace your sofa with storage space. The boxes are available with open shelves, doors, and drawers as well as optional feet. The wraparound configuration works best with a plain, straight-lined sofa. Or omit the side pieces and construct a credenza that sits behind the sofa.

>>READER TIP

My daughter's solution to the problem of paper clutter is to use baskets to collect the stacks. Then she takes the basket with her and sorts and tosses while watching TV.

Rosemarie Livings
Vero Beach, Florida

Modular Solutions

Contain the living room clutter in a coffee table and cabinet composed of cubes. Choose a mixture of forms—drawers, doors, and open shelves—to provide storage options for items you want to hide and objects you don't mind showing off. Mixing blond and ebony finishes for the coffee table reinforces this room's warm neutral color scheme. The units are screwed together through the sides and topped with heavy glass to ensure perfect alignment. Stack units vertically to form a cabinet for stashing (and organizing) more stuff.

Bookcase Essentials

Treat your bookcases as decorative spaces as well as storage, and you'll banish visual and physical clutter. Using neutral containers and binders for photo albums, scrapbooks, and mementos creates a visually calming effect. If you can build in bookcases, carry them across the top of doorways (opposite below) and consider lining an inside wall with them as well. To create a built-in look without remodeling, butt two freestanding bookcases together in a corner (opposite above). Group items by light or dark to give each shelf a consistent look. Offer the eye a resting place with a focal point on each shelf.

Another option for magazine storage: Buy metal magazine bins and hang them on the wall.

Bookshelves, whether built-in, wall-mounted, or freestanding, store a lot of stuff but can become cluttered eyesores if you're not careful. Use baskets or attractive boxes to corral papers, videos, and CDs. If these containers are on open shelves, they become a decorative element, contributing to the overall look of the room. Choose baskets to match your style—wire mesh for industrial chic, woven sea grass or wicker for casual contemporary, or ebony-stained wood for an Asian or traditional style. Select containers that match: An eclectic hodgepodge will create visual clutter that undermines your efforts.

Sort through your book collection periodically to weed out volumes you aren't likely to reread or refer to and donate them to your library or to a thrift shop. Use the freed-up space to arrange the shelves attractively, showcasing framed photos or decorative objects between groups of books.

Clean out your video collection the same way. If you haven't watched a video in a couple of years, give it away or sell it.

▶▶READER TIP

As a clutterbug who never picked up after herself and never had "a place for everything," I can tell you that deciding on the proper easy-access spot for things is the key to decluttering. Now every time I walk into a room, I put five things back where they belong. Once you master the clutter, the cleaning is a breeze!

P. S. Don't be afraid to store things where you can't see them. I used to have books to return to the library sitting on the counter and reminders tacked up to the doors, fridge, etc. Now I have a master to-do list and keep everything behind closed doors. With my list I can find things, and I don't feel overwhelmed.

Laurie Moore
Sumner, Washington

If you add wall-mounted shelves, position them so they relate to the architecture of the room—for example, between a pair of windows or in an alcove beside a fireplace—or to a major piece of furniture, such as a credenza. Otherwise they'll look like an afterthought and won't contribute to the overall harmony of the room. Also anchor them securely to wall studs using screws long enough to extend 1½ inches into the stud. If you have a 12-inch-long shelf filled with hardcover books, the books may weigh about 40 pounds.

What other papers pile up on your living room surfaces? If this is where you bring mail or your children's homework to review, set up a mini home office. Create a coffee table using storage cubes or use a side table to hold file boxes or a letter sorter. A small chest of drawers also makes a good side table that can double as file cabinet and storage space. Keep a wastebasket beside your chair, too, and go through the mail every

Shaped Bookcases

Take advantage of unusual spaces to install bookcases for storage and display. Make better use of the stairway wall with a custom-built unit that is essentially three bookcases of staggered height (below). Carve out a niche for the sofa with a combination of wall-hung open shelves and glass-front cabinets (opposite top). Or for a more temporary solution, create a wall unit by mixing a variety of modular units (opposite below). Lay laminated shelving across the units to provide a work surface or another area for display.

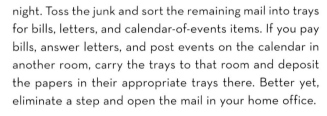

Uncluttered Collections

Clutter isn't just about the stuff that needs to be put away or thrown away. Collections you love can create visual chaos too. Turn them into eye-pleasing focal points by massing like items: Fill clear glass vases from a hobby store with vintage billiard balls or bingo balls and display old timepieces on simple wood brackets painted to match the wall. Wine corks inscribed with the date of opening recall special events.

night. Toss the junk and sort the remaining mail into trays for bills, letters, and calendar-of-events items. If you pay bills, answer letters, and post events on the calendar in another room, carry the trays to that room and deposit the papers in their appropriate trays there. Better yet, eliminate a step and open the mail in your home office.

Collect reading glasses, pens or pencils, and the television guide and remote controls in a basket or tray beside your reading chair; the tray makes items accessible yet organized. Or stow the essentials out of sight in the drawer of a side table. If the drawer of the side table is stuffed with expired coupons, unlabeled photos, and old newsletters, clean it out while you're watching TV.

Look for double-duty furniture: Ottomans with hinged lids can store toys or an afghan; a large, flat-topped wicker basket can serve as a coffee table and storage for items you only need seasonally—winter bedding, slipcovers, or holiday decorations, for example.

>>READER TIP

When my two adult children were little, we played a game called "Keep or Chuck!" We'd carry two big boxes from room to room (Mom and Dad played too), taking turns holding up items that were on the floor or cluttering the place up. Everyone voted whether to keep or chuck. The owner had final decision rights, but three "Chucks!" usually won out. At the end of the game, the "Keeps" were put away, and the "Chucks" were either tossed or given to our church thrift shop. When we were done, we ordered pizza. I'm 64 now and live alone, and I still have a "Keep or Chuck" day now and then, complete with pizza!

Barbara Scarpato
Birdsboro, Pennsylvania

Architectural Statement

Let's face it: The television is usually the true focal point of the family room. To tone down its visual impact and clean up the look of your room, tie the TV into the architecture with cabinetry. Pocket doors in a maple cabinet (opposite) pull forward to hide the TV when it's not in use. The grid of doors (above) hides a large-screen television, audio and video equipment, and a collection of videotapes, CDs, and DVDs. When the doors are closed, the unit forms a stair-stepped wall with space for display. Whether you buy ready-made cabinets, have them built, or build them yourself, plan to position the TV so your line of sight falls just below the center of the screen. Leave space at the back of the cabinets for ventilation and wiring.

Clutter isn't always caused by too much stuff. Sometimes it's the cumulative result of family members not putting things back where they belong. After a Sunday afternoon at home with a 4-year-old, this family finds its living room full of shoes, toys, games, magazines, and half-eaten snacks.

The solution is obvious: Create better places to stash things. Use a trunk instead of a coffee table, as shown here, to hide toys or throws for snuggling on winter evenings. To make accessing the contents easy, keep accessories on the trunk to a minimum.

If the sofa pillows always end up on the floor, you have too many. Keep enough to add comfort to the sofa or chair—if they're needed for back support, for example—and give away the rest.

Here the bookshelf gets a facelift with denim-covered boxes to corral small items. The boxes coordinate with the sofa fabric and provide large color blocks to focus the eye. Now the vases and framed picture actually can be seen and enjoyed instead of disappearing into the clutter.

Key Ideas at Work:

> Replace a standard coffee table with a flat-topped trunk to hold children's toys, extra blankets, or seasonal slipcovers. Use wire baskets to keep magazines and reading material in one place.

> Replace an end table with a nightstand that has a drawer. Set baskets on the nightstand shelves to organize newspapers, videotapes, and CDs. Stash remote controls in the drawer or collect them in a small basket.

> Use a picnic basket beside a chair for needlework projects or small toys.

> Tidy bookshelves so they can function as decorative focal points. Treat books, boxes, and accessories as blocks of color and arrange them in an orderly pattern that moves your eye from shelf to shelf.

BEFORE

AFTER

AFTER

AFTER

Uncluttered Decorating

Tame the visual clutter in rooms by downplaying pattern and eliminating strongly contrasting colors. Checks and florals at the window, on the coffee table, in the pillows, and on the sofa and chairs (below) give this room a busy feeling. Reupholstering or slipcovering the furniture in plain white fabric, replacing the pillows with toned-down prints, and changing the curtains to white sheers quiets the visual noise and allows the room to breathe. Dressing up the bookcase with doors further reduces visual clutter; adding a window seat and cornice board gives this area more architectural impact (and contributes under-the-seat storage).

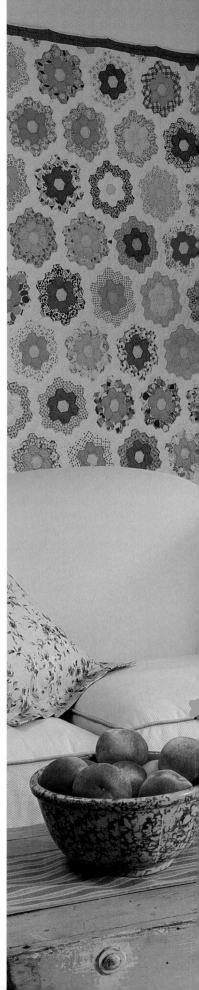

>>READER TIP

I used to save ALL of my magazines, which added up! Now when I look through a magazine, I tab the pages I want to keep. When I'm done reading, I rip out the pages I've marked and throw out the magazine. I organize the pages into folders or binders marked recipes, decorating ideas, remodeling ideas, gardening, etc. It really saves a lot of room!

Sue McNeil
Bellmore, New York

BEDROOMS

The bedroom needs to be restful and relaxing. However, it's not likely to be a haven of serenity if you drape piles of clothing over furniture, leave shoes lying on the floor, and toss spare change and jewelry on top of the dresser. Although some bedroom storage solutions require remodeling to make the most of available space, other ideas in this chapter use some inventive repurposing of items you may already have or can find at a garage sale or home improvement center.

Behind Closed Doors

A custom-built unit tucked into one side of the closet (opposite) eliminates the need for a TV stand elsewhere in the room and provides drawer space for clothing. Attached to a pullout shelf, the TV is at the right height for comfortable viewing from the bed. In addition, there's still room for hanging clothes on the other side of the closet. If you build a unit like this, be sure the electronics have adequate ventilation.

▶▶ READER TIP

I keep all the boxes that my family's new shoes come in and use them as storage boxes for other items. They stack neatly in the closet, under the bed, or anywhere else I want to put them. If you do not want to hide them, decorate the boxes with construction paper, pictures cut from magazines or comics, or cover the outside with scraps of cloth.

Melinda Calhoon
Jasper, Tennessee

To declutter your bedroom, start with the basic chore your parents assigned you as a kid: Always make your bed in the morning. An unmade bed looks messy. It only takes one or two minutes to smooth the sheets and a duvet in place and plump the pillows at the head of the bed. Get rid of the piles of decorative pillows if you don't have time to arrange them every morning.

If you drop clothes where you take them off or drape them over a chair, start training yourself to acquire some new habits. Buy an attractive fabric-lined wicker hamper and tuck it into a corner or into the closet, making it just as convenient to drop clothes there as to leave them on the floor.

Put shoes in the closet immediately. (No room in the closet? See the next chapter!) Anything that can be worn again before needing laundering or dry cleaning should go back on hangers. Do this every night for three weeks and it will become a habit. Your clothes will require less care and your room will be tidier.

Home economists recommend allowing clothing to air before putting it back in the closet. This lets body moisture absorbed by the fabric evaporate. Attach a hook or a short shelf bracket to the back of the bedroom door. Hang what you plan to wear the next day on this hook; when you come home, hang the clothing on the hook to air, then put it in the closet and bring out the next day's outfit before you go to bed. This also saves time in the morning because you won't have to agonize over what to wear and whether it's clean and in good repair.

Go through your jewelry box at least once a year. Set aside everything that's broken and not likely to get fixed, as well as earrings that lost their partners. Unless you know you're going to do something creative with this pile (such as embed the pieces in plaster of Paris on a flowerpot), toss them out. Put the pieces you wear most often and those with sentimental value in another pile.

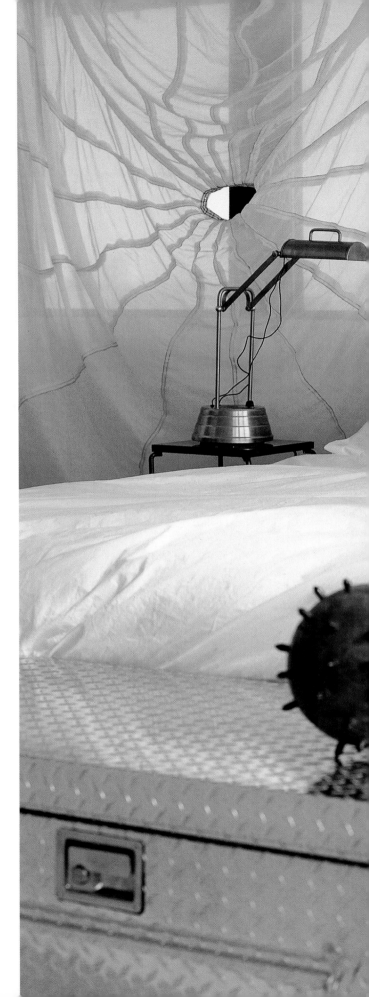

End of the Bed

If you like the clean, high-tech look of metal, shop for storage for the foot of the bed at a home improvement center or auto accessories store. An aluminum tool chest, designed to fit into a pickup truck, stores blankets, bedding, or out-of-season clothing with industrial-chic style. To make your bedroom an uncluttered haven, keep accessories to a minimum and choose clean-lined furnishings, such as metal tables and lamps (these are vintage 1920s tanning lamps).

Return these to the jewelry box. Anything you no longer wear or don't really like can go to charity or, if you have young daughters, granddaughters, nieces, or neighbors, into a dress-up box.

Every time you put away the laundry, use the opportunity to tidy dresser drawers. Consider buying clear plastic sock organizers to impose order on dresser drawers, or devise your own using narrow boxes or containers shallow enough to fit into the drawer.

Twice a year, with the change of seasons from winter to spring and fall to winter, clean out every drawer. If you can manage only one drawer an evening, that's fine. Take everything out and sort the contents into piles—need it, love it, haven't worn it in a year, and needs to be retired.

T-shirts, sweaters, and sports clothing in good condition that you haven't worn in a year can go to charity or a yard sale. Worn-out socks make good cleaning rags, so stash them with your cleaning supplies.

Vacuum the drawer to remove lint and dust. Moth larvae feed on lint, so keeping drawers clean helps prevent pest damage to clothing.

Everything that goes back into the drawer should be neatly folded—you'll get more into the drawer that way. Tuck an herbal sachet or a bar of fragrant soap (such as rose, lavender, or vetiver) into your lingerie drawer to infuse items with a pleasing fragrance.

Corral dresser-top clutter by using a container to serve as a catchall for loose change and keys. Choose

>>READER TIP

I keep my socks and pantyhose tidy with sandwich-size plastic bags. I place the socks and hosiery into the bags, sorting them by color and type in my drawer. Sockettes and knee-high nylons of the same color can be stored together to save on bags. This eliminates disarray and it protects the hosiery from snags when I open or close the drawer.

Vernamaree Nelson
Richfield, Minnesota

something that matches the colors in your room and pleases your eye—a decorative plate, a shallow brass bowl, or a vintage ashtray—for an attractive, stylish way to keep the items from your pockets in one place.

If you have perfumes and lotions on the dresser, organize them in a tray. Pulling like items together in a single container creates an island of order and makes the dresser look more organized.

Use the same trick to organize bedside tables. If you keep an alarm clock, tissues, water carafe and drinking glass, magazines, books, and reading glasses beside the bed, collect them all onto a tray for a neater look. A large bedside basket also works for keeping books and magazines at hand, but go through it periodically to clean out anything you haven't read. Otherwise it's another clutter collector.

In-Wall Storage

If space is too tight in the bedroom to allow for a freestanding lingerie chest, try stealing some footage from a closet to build an in-wall chest. Shallow drawers hold jewelry, accessories, socks, and lingerie. A small slide-out TV can fit into a niche above. Hire an electrician to run the wiring into the closet and install the electrical outlets.

Headboard with Storage

Turn ready-made shoe stackers upside down to create wall-hung shelves that serve as a bedside table. Screw the backs of the side units into wall studs to make sure the shelves are securely anchored. A wall-hung unit clears floor space, making the room feel larger and providing a location for more storage containers, such as baskets or boxes to hold books, magazines, or blankets.

To make this headboard unit, you'll need two long and two short shoe stackers, 1×12 pine, 1×2 pine, and hardboard. For each side of the bed cut a shelf from 1×12 pine the length of the long shoe stacker plus 1½ inches. Turn the stackers upside down and sandwich the shelf between, with one short edge flush with one side of the stackers. Cut two pieces of ¼-inch hardboard to fit the backs of the long and short stackers. Assemble the backing, stackers, and shelf with screws. Cut a headboard top shelf from 1×12 pine equal to the width of the mattress and both short shoe stackers, plus 3 inches for overhang. From 1×2 pine cut two side rails equal to the length of the side units and a top rail equal to the mattress width. Attach the side rails to side units and the top rail to the top shelf, securing them 2 inches in from the front edge. From ½-inch hardboard, cut a headboard that extends to the floor. Paint all pieces with white enamel. Lay the side units facedown; screw the headboard to the side rails and the top shelf to the short stackers. Secure the unit to wall studs.

>>READER TIP

I hate clutter and disorderliness, and so within my realm of living (I am 18 years old) I have made it a priority to keep my own possessions to a minimum. That means I get rid of anything I KNOW I don't need or place extreme value on. Sometimes I go through a shelf, closet, or trunk and find things I can't get rid of just yet because of their sentimental value. Then another week or two might go by and I will sort through my "sentimental pile" again, tossing things I don't need or want. When I was in kindergarten, I kept every single worksheet and paper. I have found that now when I get rid of things when I know I should, I hardly remember or care about what I threw out, and the things I keep have a much higher value to me.

Loni Hawkins
Blackfoot, Idaho

Give yourself places to put bedside necessities and keep the bedroom orderly with a double-decker bedside table. Use a coffee table as the base and stand a two-drawer storage unit from an office supply store on top. The unit can serve as a bedside medicine chest for cough drops, tissues, and aspirin. Or tuck your journal and pen, books, and magazines into the drawers to reduce visual clutter. The coffee table also provides plenty of space for a water glass and carafe, air purifier, and a lamp. A coffee table as a nightstand works best with a bed that's low, so the surface of the table is within easy reach from the bed. You probably need a taller lamp, though, to cast good light for reading.

If your bed is more traditional in style and higher off the floor, transform a narrow side table into a roomy nightstand. Use one or more two-drawer storage units on top to serve as a mini dresser or jewelry chest. Put the space below the table to work with wooden boxes or lidded baskets to store extra bedding or out-of-season clothing.

End-of-Bed Bench

Build a bookcase/bench from old fruit crates. Choose three sturdy, same-size crates, stand them on end, and screw them together through the sides. Cut a top and bottom from 1-inch boards and secure with screws. Paint as desired. To achieve a weathered, worn effect, prime and paint with a base coat of white. After the paint dries, rub a candle over the edges to resist the second coat of paint. Apply the contrasting top coat. Let dry, then sand to expose part of the base coat. Top the bench with a skirted cushion or pillows, or leave it uncovered.

Underbed Storage

Turn an old dresser drawer into underbed storage on wheels. Measure under the bed for the amount of clearance you need, then choose casters accordingly. Screw casters to the bottom corners of the drawer; drill holes in the drawer face to accept heavy rope. To form a handle, thread the ends of a length of rope through the holes; knot the ends inside the drawer.

Dresser Conversion

Create cottage-style storage from a garage-sale dresser. Remove the drawers and convert them to underbed (or under the dresser) storage (see page 57). Use ⅛-inch hardboard to create shelves in the space formerly occupied by the drawers. Give the dresser and mirror frame a weathered-paint finish following the instructions on page 56. Tuck baskets on the new shelves to hold clothes.

▶▶READER TIP

I have learned that the less stuff I have, the better my chances of maintaining an orderly environment. After I started to get rid of "stuff," I really experienced a feeling of power over my own instincts to collect and keep things. Now every time I do my seasonal closet switch-over, I consider it a badge of honor to have at least one garbage bag full of clothing and shoes to donate and one smaller bag (papers and magazines) to discard.

Beatriz Seinuk-Ackerman
New York, New York

More Options for Under the Bed

If your bed is high enough off the floor to accommodate storage containers, put this space to work. Containers with lids will protect items from dust. Build your own drawer on wheels (below) from ³/₄-inch plywood and add a lid cut from ¹/₄-inch plywood or hardboard. Sew soft-sided fabric containers in any size that fits your underbed storage space (right) using heavy quilted fabric, grommets, and fabric ties. Add a fabric handle on one end or side so you can pull the container out easily. To store small items, use vintage or new hatboxes (below right) or baskets (opposite).

▶▶READER TIPS

I put all my sheets in underbed containers and slide them under the bed in the guest room. This frees up closet space!

Christine Elsfelder
Sparks, Nevada

Fold T-shirts and sweatshirts and stack them vertically in the drawers instead of laying them flat. It's easier to find the one you want and keeps you from repeatedly wearing only the ones "on top."

Becky Aylor
Sisters, Oregon

Bin There, Done That

Make it easy for kids to put away their toys. Collapsible storage cubes with mesh sides are lightweight and see-through and tuck neatly away on extra-deep laminate shelves. Bins with lids are good for puzzles, games, and toys with lots of parts. Label opaque bins so you'll know what's inside. For safety, anchor the shelving unit to the wall with L brackets. They come in various sizes, so you can use them even with shelves that set away from the wall.

- -

▶▶READER TIP

I use the large gift tins (usually filled with popcorn or pretzels) to hold one year's worth of magazines for two or three different subscriptions. The magazines curve to fit the container. After I put the lid on, I cover the tin with a scarf or luncheon tablecloth and use the container as a plant stand.

Darlene Snow
Clinton, Missouri

Kids' rooms become subject to massive amounts of clutter because this is where they sleep and often where they play, study, and dress. Encourage tidy habits by example and training and by providing storage systems that make staying organized easier. Involve them in the decluttering efforts—after all, it's their room and they have to live with the results.

Play the professional organizer with your kids: Ask them what they like about the way their room is arranged and what is stored there. Is it working for them? Could some things be better stored somewhere else? If they don't use the closet or hangers, what would make it easier for them? Are shelves better than hangers? And the really tough question: What are they not wearing, playing with, or using that could be given away?

As with any room, evaluate what you need to store before investing in storage containers or shelving systems. A toddler's toys may require a large basket or plastic tubs, while an older child's games, collections, and hobbies may call for stackable lidded boxes, stacked plastic drawers on wheels (intended for home offices), or open shelving.

Use the space under the bed to store extra bedding, sports equipment, and out-of-season clothing. Or shop for a bed that incorporates storage drawers below the bed frame.

Children start learning to name colors around the age of 2 or 3, so use color coding to teach your tots to put away toys, clothes, and books. Buy plastic bins or boxes in bright colors and designate one color to store each type of item: blue for balls, orange for trucks and cars, and yellow for shoes. Tape a picture of the item on the front of the bin and make cleanup a game.

Set aside a couple of hours to go through toy boxes and the closet with your children to evaluate what needs to be kept, tossed, or donated to charity.

To keep crayons, puzzles, and toys with small parts from getting lost, sort them into plastic drawer organizers

intended for flatware and caddies used for cleaning supplies. Store them on shelves out of the reach of younger children.

Keep a laundry basket in each child's room to collect dirty clothing. When you do laundry, the basket can go straight to the laundry room and return full of clean, folded clothes. If your kids live out of the laundry basket, consider replacing the dresser with cupboards specially built to accommodate the laundry baskets. Fill one or two with folded, clean clothes. As children work their way through the basket, have them toss dirty clothes into the empty basket. When it's full, the basket goes to the laundry. If the baskets are attractive, you won't need to put doors on the cupboards.

Adapt closet space so children can access their own clothes—lower the rod to their eye level and install shelves across one end of the closet to hold toys, games, shoes, or clothing. If everything your children use or wear is stored within reach, it will be easier for items to go back where they belong rather than on the floor. On the shelves above, you can store sheets and blankets or out-of-season clothing—items that aren't accessed often.

Space Savers

Wall-mounted shelves provide storage without taking up floor space, and a twin bed with a trundle beneath doesn't gobble up room the way a full-size or even a bunk bed does. For sleepovers, pull out the trundle; this one is built-in (see page 188 for sources), but you also can buy a metal pop-up trundle frame to slide under any bed with adequate clearance. A chest at the end of the bed can store bedding— or sleeping bags for more sleepover guests.

▶▶READER TIP

I use a medium-size plastic garbage can as a bedside table and store out-of-season clothes inside. I've topped it with a round piece of wood from the hardware store and a floor-length tablecloth with a piece of round glass over the cloth. I change the tablecloth with the seasons too.

Eileen Stroud
Severna Park, Maryland

Hang It Up

Wall pockets let kids store their toys in plain sight and at a level they easily can reach. Make a wall hanging of sturdy fabric, such as denim or painter's canvas, to hold heavier items such as polymer clay and paints (above). Install grommets along the top edge to hang on wall hooks. Shape the pockets to fit specific kinds of objects and reinforce the bottom of pockets with cardboard to hold bulky items (above). Pockets stitched to a bed skirt (opposite) keep books for bedtime reading and favorite stuffed toys handy and off the floor. For a nursery, use a wall hanging with pockets (left) to keep essentials close to where you need them. The peg rack holder adapts to other uses as the child grows.

A Place for Everything

When you're trying to control clutter in kids' rooms, providing a place for everything allows for the possibility that everything will find its place. Bookshelves are a must, but even a wagon can corral a herd of stuffed animals (opposite). A utility cabinet on wheels has drawers and shelves to accommodate models, collections, and hobby supplies.

CLOSETS

It's easy for closets to become dens of messiness because you can close the door and not have to look at the chaos—until it's time to get dressed the next day. The rewards of a tidy closet go beyond the serenity and sense of control you achieve anytime you declutter an area. Properly stored clothes and shoes last longer and keep their shape better. Plus, with an orderly closet, you'll know what you have, so you won't buy duplicates of items by mistake.

If you've reached the point where the hangers in your closet have no more room to slide along the rod, it's time for action. Set aside about two hours to thoroughly clean out and organize one closet. First, take everything out—all clothes, shoes, and whatever else has found its way into the recesses of the space. This may expose some dust bunnies, so vacuum the floor and shelves before starting the sorting process.

Take an honest look at every item of clothing. Is it in good condition? Do you like it? Have you worn it in the last year? Does it look good on you? Does it fit well? If you can answer yes to all of those questions, hang the item (temporarily) in the closet. If you answer no to any of them, put it aside to give to charity or sell in a yard sale—unless it's torn, stained, worn-out, or in such poor condition that no one else will want it. In that case, put it in a garbage bag.

After you've weeded out the items you no longer wear or need, go back through and check to see that the keepers combine into useable outfits. Then sort them by season. Make sure the out-of-season clothes are clean and pack them away in garment bags.

Depending on what works best for you, organize in-season clothes by length (dresses, pants, and long skirts; suits, jackets, short skirts, and blouses); by color; or by purpose (business, casual, and evening wear). Sort ties by color and hang them on an over-the-door hanger.
Use the same process to go through your shoes, tossing

Dream Closet

If you could turn a whole bedroom into a dressing room, perhaps it would look like this. But even if you're working on a smaller scale, you can borrow the idea of bookcase-style shelves and drawer/shelf combinations to hold purses and shoes and clear bins for folded shirts and tops. Some professional organizers recommend hanging clothes by color rather than by type (business versus casual) because dress codes tend to blur the lines between the two.

Walk-In Master Closet

Line your master closet with cedar, then add these clutter-buster components: a built-in maple chest (above left and right) with divided drawers for lingerie and shelves for bulky sweaters; a cabinet for boots, gloves, scarves, and accessories (left); top-to-bottom tilted shelving for shoes; shelving for handbags and hats; and full-height and double-hung clothes rods (opposite). As you plan your closet design, remember you'll need 20 inches of rod length for every 10 shirts or blouses. Double-hung rods should be installed at 36 to 42 inches above the floor and 76 to 84 inches above the floor. A full-height closet rod should be 65 to 69 inches above the floor and 12 to 14 inches away from the back wall for standard-size hangers.

>> R E A D E R   T I P

To declutter your closet, throw away anything that doesn't fit properly. If you lose weight, you can treat yourself to some new clothes. Throw away anything faded, even if it was your favorite comfy shirt. I found that when I take clothes out of the closet and vow to have a yard sale or give them to charity, it never gets done. It's all too easy to go back through the box a year or so later and start pulling things out like it's Christmas morning! Get it out of the house.

Jill Snyder
Koshkonong, Missouri

Built-In Options

Double-hung rods make the best use of space when the clothes are shirts, jackets, and pants folded over suit-pant hangers (left). Hooks on the inside of the double doors hold ties and belts, and shoe cubbies stacked behind the doorjamb store shoes. Another handy item to incorporate in the closet is a dresser with open shelves, a drawer that locks to protect valuables, and pullout wire baskets to presort laundry (opposite).

any worn-out or out-of-style pairs. The easiest way to keep shoes in good condition is to return them to their boxes after you take them off. If you haven't kept the boxes, bring in a shoe rack or low shelving unit to keep them organized and off the floor. Piling shoes on top of each other creates chaos and it risks scratching or scuffing the leather uppers. Arrange shoes by purpose—formal, work, casual, and athletic—to make it easier to find the pair you need.

To build your own closet system from ready-to-assemble parts (available at home centers and discount stores), organize your clothes by length. How many long dresses, skirts, and pairs of pants do you have? Measure the amount of pole length they'll require and allow that much space for a full-length section of the system. If most or all of your wardrobe consists of half-length items (jackets, short skirts, blouses, or shirts), you can install two rods. Or use the extra space under a single rod for shelves, a small bookcase, or a small chest to hold sweaters, jeans, shorts, T-shirts, or shoes.

Maximize the top shelf in a closet with stackable plastic drawers that can hold handbags, athletic clothes, and extra bedding. To make access more convenient, buy a lightweight, two-step ladder that folds flat and hang it on a hook on the inside of the closet door.

Storage Tips for Clothing

Don't hang wool sweaters, knitted dresses, shawls, and jackets. They'll stretch out of shape. Instead, fold them and store them flat in drawers or on closet shelves.

Use padded hangers for delicate fabrics such as silk, lace, and linen. Wooden or heavy-duty plastic hangers preserve the shape of clothes better than wire.

Remove clothing from dry cleaning bags immediately. Leaving it in the bags can trap humidity and cause yellowing. If you have dresses or suits that need to be protected from dust, hang them in zippered wardrobe bags made for that purpose.

Before storing seasonal clothing (or longer-term items—such as wedding dresses or christening dresses), have them dry cleaned or laundered according to the manufacturer's recommendations. Even if an item appears to be clean, there may be stains or soil that will discolor the outfit in storage and permanently damage the fabric. Residual stains also will attract pests.

Because fabric needs to breathe, don't store it in airtight plastic containers for long periods; instead, use fabric bags or garment bags with breathable gussets. Or wrap the clothing in old bedsheets to protect it from dust.

Wrap keepsake children's clothing in acid-free tissue paper and store it in a cedar chest or a trunk. For long-term storage, keep clothing (and any other fabric item) out of direct sunlight and in a moderate environment (about 65 to 70 degrees). Avoid storing clothing in a damp basement or an uninsulated attic.

To protect clothing from moths, ask the dry cleaner to use a cleaning solution that includes a moth-proofing agent. Moth larvae (which do the damage) are attracted to residual food stains, perspiration, or urine rather than to clean wool. Moths also attack fur, feathers, silk, and cotton. Although cedar blocks and cedar chips don't protect against moths, the cedar oil in cedar-lined closets and chests may kill young larvae. Lightly sand the wood every year or two to release fresh oil.

▶▶READER TIP

I am a clutter magnet, but one trick that works for me is: "In with the new, out with the old." Every time I buy an item (other than groceries), I get rid of something comparable that I can do without. If I buy a new blouse or T-shirt or jeans, I take an old piece of clothing that I don't wear or don't like or that doesn't fit and throw it out, put it in the ragbag, or put it in my charity donation box. If I'm feeling really good, I get rid of two, maybe three items while I'm at it.

Yolanda Goynes
George West, Texas

Design Details

Take advantage of a 3-inch-deep space to add hooks for scarves (opposite left). It may seem like a little thing, but professional organizer Kasey Vejar from Shawnee Mission, Kansas, insists that "hangers are 50 percent of getting the closet organized. You want hangers that are good for the clothing and look nice." Although she recommends wood or heavy-duty plastic hangers, some organizers will accept well-made wire hangers too (opposite right). Use a vintage drapery tieback turned vertically to keep purses in one place (right).

Yikes! Help needed here! Although this teenager's walk-in closet was roomy, it wasn't well designed for her needs. Dirty clothes ended up on the floor because she was using the container for the hamper as a side table in the bedroom. An overabundance of rod space and shoe storage made the closet inefficient. "The bedroom is small," says professional organizer Kasey Vejar of Shawnee Mission, Kansas, "so we wanted to move all of her dressing-related items into the closet and make it an all-in-one dressing room."

Kasey recommends custom-closet modules sold at home improvement centers. They're reasonably priced, available in a variety of colors, and offer a range of mix-and-match elements such as shelves, baskets, and drawers. To keep dirty clothes off the floor, Kasey introduced a collapsible fabric hamper. When it's full, it can go straight to the laundry room.

To help make the space seem larger in this closet, Kasey painted the trim white and bought white modular units.

In addition, using a single type of hanger makes the closet look neat and organized. Kasey recommends white plastic hangers for shirts, heavy-duty plastic or wooden hangers for jeans and pants, and wooden hangers for fine clothing. For skirts use hangers with clips.

Key Ideas at Work:

➤ Add double rods for short items, with space for a few longer items, to consolidate the clothes in a more efficient area.

➤ A tower with drawers can provide space for pajamas, socks, and underwear. To organize shoes, Kasey bought two stacking units, one with a grid and one with shelves (see page 82). This works well for shoes now and can be used for other items if needs change later.

➤ Replace standard 12-inch-wide shelves with 16-inch shelving, which better accommodates boxes and tubs used for storing out-of-season clothing or hobby supplies.

➤ Sort items by color. "It's very pleasing to the eye to see the rainbow of color," says Kasey. The color blocks look neat, and that will encourage you to keep the closet tidy.

BEFORE

BEFORE

Key Ideas at Work:

> Kasey recommends plastic hangers with hooks for hanging shirts or tank tops with spaghetti straps. Hang jeans on heavy-duty plastic hangers.

> Every year when switching out seasonal clothes, purge old or worn-out items.

> Keep purses and bags on an accessible shelf or hang them on a "chain gang," a plastic chain with heavy-duty clips that is suspended from the rod. You also can use metal chain from a hardware store.

AFTER

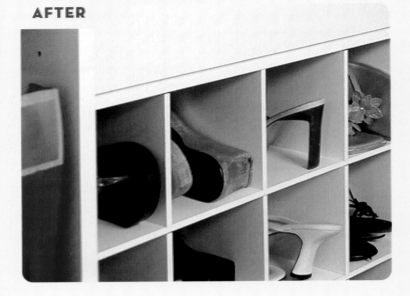

AFTER

AFTER

AFTER

AFTER

It's OK to throw out empty boxes. Part of the problem in this boy's bedroom was that one closet stored empty computer boxes. Although manufacturers recommend that you keep the original box in case you need to ship the equipment for repair, it's better to knock down the box and store it flattened in a basement or utility room. Don't let it take up valuable space in the bedroom.

The bedroom has two small closets, each fitted with a rod and shelf, but the teen used only part of one closet for clothing. A corner of one closet housed sports equipment. His media equipment and games were scattered around the room or filling the bookcase, so he had no place to put his books.

Kasey Vejar began by "purging and sorting," which included getting rid of empty boxes. To make the second closet more functional and better suited to his needs, she removed the rod and installed floor-to-ceiling adjustable shelving. A collapsible fabric hamper tucked into one closet makes it easy to keep dirty clothes off the floor.

Kasey transferred the cords, cables, and wiring into a single container in the closet. Software and games were placed in easy-access containers on the closet shelves, so the bookcase can accommodate books.

Key Ideas at Work:

> Don't limit yourself to the usual closet structure of rod and shelf if it doesn't meet your needs. This teenager needed storage more than hanging space, so Kasey installed adjustable shelves that can be removed to reinstall the rod later if needed.

> Organize T-shirts, which are easier to access if folded on shelves, by shelf dividers instead of putting them in a drawer.

> Overdoor hooks and organizers keep backpacks, belts, and baseball caps tidy in space that normally is wasted.

> Store DVDs, baseball cards, golf supplies, and other small items in containers so they are easy to find. Often-accessed items can be placed in unlidded plastic containers. Put items that aren't used as often into lidded, labeled boxes.

BEFORE **BEFORE**

AFTER

AFTER

AFTER

Cabana Bookshelf

Wrap a plain bookcase in a bedsheet to create a freestanding closet. Tie back the "doors" to show off an attractive arrangement of objects, or let them drop to cover up what is stored behind them.

To make this project, you'll need a 32×13×69 pine shelf unit, two king-size cotton sheets, 10 yards of 1½-inch-wide white grosgrain ribbon, a thick rubber band, an empty paint or coffee can, and two large grommets. Let out the top wide cuff on each sheet and rehem by folding under the edge ¼ inch twice and stitching. Place the sheets right sides together, aligning one side and the rehemmed end. (If the sheets don't match on the other edges, trim to the smaller size.) Stitch on three sides, leaving the rehemmed edge open. Turn and press. Stitch grosgrain ribbon along the front edges. Drape the curtain over the bookshelf with the hem at the bottom (above left). Gather at the top with the rubber band and rest it on top of the can to make a peak (left). Fold and tuck the fabric ends to make a rosette. For tiebacks, install grommets two-thirds of the way from the floor and 16 inches in from the edge. Thread a 2-yard length of ribbon through each and tie in a bow (above).

Organization is essential for a multipurpose closet. This utility closet had one set of 24×24-inch-deep shelves, an area for hanging clothes, and a set of project drawers, but the storage space wasn't accessible. The shelves, suitable for storing luggage and large boxes, were inadequate for linens, cleaning supplies, and household items.

Professional organizer Barbara Brock of New York City helped the owner sort through everything in the closet and identify a list of needs: places to hang guests' clothing and seasonal clothing; storage for bed linens, bath towels, and cleaning products; and a spot for gift wrap, hardware supplies, and paper items. She then divided the closet, dedicating one end to guest/bath/linens and the other to cleaning/project items.

Replacing the 24-inch shelves with 14-inch-deep ones provided space for linens, towels, and cleaning supplies and opened room to walk into the closet. Screws or hooks inserted into predrilled holes in the shelving hold the vacuum hose, brooms, dusters, and dust pan. Items previously in drawers were sorted into bins and labeled.

Barbara recommends designating certain areas for specific uses to ensure that the supplies or items related to that function are where you need them when you need them (provided you always remember to put them away). In this closet a set of utility drawers houses hardware and gift wrap supplies. In the hardware drawer an expandable cutlery tray separates tools. (For product information, see page 189.)

Key Ideas at Work:

➤ Designate one end of the closet for clothing, linens, and towels. Install double-hung rods to accommodate shirts, jackets, and folded pants. Choose a modular system that allows for narrow towers of adjustable shelves.

➤ Use hooks to hang mops, the dust pan, and other cleaning equipment. Keep items off the floor by hanging them on a wall or other vertical surface to save space.

➤ Use different but coordinating bins to corral supplies. Label bins for easy access.

➤ Organize gift-wrapping supplies, batteries, and gift cards with trays that fit onto a wall-hung grid. A waist-high unit provides a work surface and accommodates the shallow plastic drawers this owner was using before along the back wall.

➤ If space is at a premium, consider replacing a large vacuum cleaner with a space-saving smaller model.

BEFORE

BEFORE

AFTER

AFTER

AFTER

BATHS

Ah, the uncluttered bathroom—the spa-like retreat where you soak away stress at the end of the day. Not at your house, you say? Efficient, attractive storage may not transform your bathroom into a soothing oasis, but it can make the space look tidier, which will make you feel more serene. And if you can find your brush or razor without rooting through assorted toiletries, you'll start the day in a much better frame of mind.

Pole Power

Take advantage of unused air space by installing chrome poles that can be fitted with an array of accessories, from makeup mirrors to towel racks and shelves. Check bath stores or home improvement centers for them. In this small remodeled bath, separate vanities designed to suit the individual heights of the homeowners stop short of the floor, making the space seem larger. (The mirrored wall helps too.)

To bring order to the bathroom, tackle one clutter-magnet area at a time: the medicine chest, vanity drawers, and undersink cabinets are the most likely suspects. Throw out expired over-the-counter medicines and contact cleaning solutions along with nearly empty bottles of cough syrup or cold medicine.

Toss old makeup. Color preferences change and makeup can become a breeding ground for fungus and bacteria. Mascara starts to dry out after about three months; eyeliners, eye shadow, and concealers need replacing after three to six months. If you've had lipstick longer than a year, throw it away. Liquid- and powder-based foundation should be good for two years, but blush should be replaced after six months. Nail polish, if properly stored, can last two years.

Those little bottles of lotion and shampoo from hotels are great for traveling, but do you really need to keep 25 or 30 of them? Commit to using them—don't buy another regular-size bottle of shampoo or hand lotion until they're gone. Or consolidate the contents into one clear plastic bottle (travel-size containers are available at discount stores and drugstores) and throw the little bottles away. If you have a collection of unopened little bottles, donate them to a homeless shelter.

How many cleaners do you have stashed under the sink? How many do you use? Narrow the collection to one or two, such as a general-purpose spray cleaner or nonabrasive cleaner that cuts through soap scum and grime and a mild bleaching agent to cut mildew. Use liquid chlorine bleach to remove mildew stains from caulk and grout. If you clean the bathroom weekly, a mixture of 1 part white vinegar and 2 parts water will cut soap film, mineral deposits, sticky dirt, and hard-water stains. Use baking soda mixed with enough water to

In-Wall Storage

If your remodeling or building plans include a bathroom with a separate area for the vanity, consider allowing space in the intervening privacy wall for towel cubbies and shadowbox shelves. With this arrangement, pretty towels become part of the color scheme. The shadowbox openings become the spot of choice for attractive toiletries and accessories.

‐‐

➤➤READER TIP

I usually keep only two or three cleaners in my house. Although it's tempting to buy the flashy new cleaners that come on the market, I know the old standbys are tried and true. I save money and avoid the clutter of lots of different containers.

Jill Snyder
Koshkonong, Missouri

obtain the consistency of peanut butter to scrub sinks, bathtubs, and countertops. (Homemade cleaners aren't strong enough to tackle accumulated grime, however.)

For quick jobs, keep a cleaning rag and a pair of latex gloves under the sink with the cleaners. If you have small children, use childproof safety latches on cabinet doors.

Sort under-the-sink items by type—household cleaning supplies, paper products, and personal-care products—then place each group into a plastic bin or tub. Make better use of the space under the sink with shelf helpers or plastic-coated wire racks sold in the kitchen section of organization and container stores. A plastic-coated wire rack (designed for kitchen cabinets) can be attached to the inside of the undersink cabinet door to store cleaning supplies or extra personal-care products.

Keep vanity drawers tidy by sorting makeup, medicines, and toiletries into plastic or metal-mesh containers such as those sold for holding cutlery or office supplies. A combination of square and rectangular containers should fit into your drawers as neatly as jigsaw puzzle pieces.

In the medicine cabinet, cluster makeup brushes, mascara, and lipstick pencils into a single container, such as a small cream pitcher or wide-mouth vase. They'll take up less space, and you can find what you need quickly. Little clay flowerpots corral tube medicines so you don't end up buying duplicates. Check a home improvement center for a small chest with drawers for holding screws and nails—the drawers can just as easily store bathroom odds and ends, such as hairpins, emery boards, and razor blades.

Although you'll want to keep shampoo, body wash, and facial cleansers in the shower or at the tub where you use them, stash makeup and other personal-care items in vanity drawers or the medicine cabinet. When

More In-Wall Storage

If you can borrow space from an adjacent closet, consider building a chest of drawers into the wall (opposite). Installed right beside the bathtub, the drawers put bath supplies and towels within easy reach. Even the 4-inch-deep space between studs can provide useful bathroom storage (left). Open shelves are easier to build than cupboards or drawers (below); keep them tidy with labeled, canvas-lined baskets.

countertops are relatively bare, the room will look serenely uncluttered.

If you're squeezed for towel-hanging space, install a row of pegs behind the door or look for a pole-type towel holder to stand in a corner.

Go through towels once a year and weed out the ragged and old ones. Add these to your ragbag. Organize the remaining bath towels, hand towels, and washcloths into sets so when you want a fresh set, they're all together. If you don't have a linen closet or shelf space in the bathroom, store towels and washcloths in a chest of drawers in the hall just outside the bathroom.

Avoid buying duplicate or triplicate items by setting aside an area for refills. Whether it's under the sink or in a deep vanity drawer, use this space as your pantry for extra soap, contact solution, shaving cream, toilet paper, and shampoo. When it's time to replace an item, check the pantry.

Vanity, Vanity

Use a silver serving tray to organize beauty and bath supplies in one convenient place (below). Put cotton balls, bath beads, and cotton swabs in attractive glass canisters or lidded jars so they're practical and pretty. If you have space in the bathroom, add a desklike vanity separate from the sink (opposite) to keep clutter away from the sink area and give you a place to sit while doing your hair or nails.

- -

▶▶READER TIP

I purchased small plastic boxes with handles and placed them in my bathroom drawers to hold lotions, cosmetics, hair accessories, etc. When I need to put on makeup or fix my hair, I lift the box out of the drawer and set it on top of the counter, then return it to the drawer when I'm finished.

Marcia Calcaterra
Washington, Michigan

Adaptive Reuse

A vintage dentist's cabinet works well for bathroom storage (opposite). A small bench turned upside down and mounted on the wall (above left) makes an unusual bathroom shelf; attach a towel bar to its top for hand towels. Add a plate rail with pegs (below left) for hanging jewelry or towels. Use vintage tin picnic baskets to store extra bath linens (above).

▶▶READER TIP

To keep sunblock and bug spray handy, I use the cute silverware and napkin caddies that usually come as a set with tumblers and pitchers. Everyone knows right away where the sprays can be found, and there's no messy clutter of bottles lying around.

Dana Gizzi
Canfield, Ohio

HOME OFFICES

Whether your home office is command central for running a business or the collection point for all paperwork related to running a home, it needs to be organized and orderly. Otherwise you could forget to pay bills and lose important papers. If your office is also a guest bedroom, hobby room, or a corner of the kitchen or family room, being organized is even more important to safeguard your records and paperwork from other types of clutter.

To begin decluttering, sort everything into three piles: "related to housekeeping or home business," "belongs somewhere else," and "needs to be tossed or given away." Once you've eliminated the "belongs somewhere else" and "needs to be tossed" piles, you're ready to start weeding out and sorting the home office stuff. (You can either deal with the "belongs somewhere else" pile first or save it until you conquer the clutter in the office, which will motivate you to move on to the next space. If the "needs to be tossed" pile includes records or papers with personal information, shred them before throwing away or recycling.)

Consider what needs to be stored before you buy containers. If you have lots of supplies (pens, paper clips, blank CDs, and printer cartridges, for example), gather them in shallow boxes. Clear plastic bins let you see the contents. If you prefer the look of metal, woven baskets, or cloth-covered boxes, use labels to identify the contents so you can quickly find what you need. Store fresh paper and envelopes in flat, open baskets so you don't have to remove a box or bin lid every time you need to refill the printer.

To keep your paperwork in order, sort papers by categories you'll remember and slot them into labeled file folders. How should you name your categories? Use the first words that come to you when you look at the paperwork: automobile maintenance or car repair? Health insurance or doctor's bill? Using the term you're most likely to think of will help you find the folders without wasting time searching.

Which paperwork do you need to keep and for how long? See the list on page 125 for the major categories affecting most people. If you run a business out of your home, you have to retain the paperwork that enables you to maintain the business. Your tax adviser can help

>>READER TIP

Someone suggested this to me a long time ago, and I've found it works. When I am in a clutter-banishing mode, I pack stuff I think I want to let go into boxes. I label the box with the date and put the box in the basement. If I come across this box more than a year later and I still haven't opened it, I let it go immediately—WITHOUT OPENING IT. Open it and you have to start all over. I figure if I haven't missed whatever is in the box for a year, I don't need it.

Miriam Kearney
Stirling, Ontario, Canada

Creative Shelving

Turn a sliver of space into an office: Bring in a worktable and hang vintage fruit crates above it for bookshelves with retro character. Choose sturdy fruit crates, reinforcing the sides and bottom with screws, if necessary, to make sure they can bear the weight of books. Attach the crates to wall studs with screws, positioning the lower crate high enough to clear your computer.

Office Help

Emphasize the "home" in "home office" with repurposed accessories and furniture that offer comfortable style as well as efficient function. A muffin tin (left) keeps small office supplies organized and accessible. An armoire (opposite) fitted with shelves and a slide-out tray for the keyboard looks like a wardrobe when you close the doors.

you decide which tax-related papers to keep and for how long. Also check with your tax adviser about laws regarding the home office deduction and whether your office space can be used for both personal and business purposes. If not, you may need to set aside a file cabinet in another part of the house for household records.

What's your filing style? If you like papers out of sight, opt for file cabinets. If you work best with stacks and like to have files out where you can see them (and therefore remember to deal with them), look for containers deep enough to stand file folders upright in them. Place the containers within easy reach of your desk. If you have only 6 to 10 working files, look for stepped file organizers at office supply stores. Or save tabletop space and assemble a wall-hung unit with plastic or Euro-style metal pockets for files.

Keep a folder for "matters pending"—such as catalog orders you've placed, airline tickets, hotel reservations, and car rentals—anything you have acted on that needs a response. Keeping these items in one place saves you from scrambling to find the information.

▶▶READER TIP

I quilt, embroider, and do general crafts. I also use the same space as a home office and always had a mess of little packets and plastic containers in my desk drawers for all my small supplies. It was impossible to find anything. My solution: magnetic boards hung on the wall. I glued magnets to the bottom of small disposable plastic containers (they have to be fairly lightweight) and filled them with needles, paper clips, beads, etc. Now they are at eye level, "stuck" on my magnetic board, and are very easy to grab and replace. I'm planning to put colored stickers on the tops to label and sort everything by category.

Beatriz Seinuk-Ackerman
New York, New York

Create order from chaos. The main issue for this homeowner—as for most people—was paper clutter. The file cabinet was so stuffed with old papers that the owner stopped using it. In addition, the setup of the office proved inconvenient, with inadequate lighting and a flimsy card table instead of a proper desk.

Professional organizer Kasey Vejar of Shawnee Mission, Kansas, worked with the owner to tackle the mess. "We cling to information and tend to keep papers long past their usefulness," says Kasey. Eighty percent of the papers you file you'll never touch or look at again, so as you decide whether to keep something, think about whether it's worth the space it's going to take up.

Once the homeowner purged the office of unneeded and out-of-date papers, she sorted the remainder into reference (warranties, insurance policies, investment records) and action (bills, letters, subscriptions, catalog orders). Reference papers went into new file drawers; for action papers, Kasey created a desktop sorting system, labeling folders by action: phone calls, e-mails, correspondence, purchases, online research, and so on. "Group like activities together for good time management," she advises.

"Don't feel like you have to hang on to every scrap of paper people give you," says Kasey. If it's information you can use in the next 30 to 60 days, file it in the appropriate action folder; otherwise, toss it.

Key Ideas at Work:

> Invest in a suitable desk that accommodates your work style. This L-shape modular unit with file cabinets provides plenty of work surface and storage and looks good too.

> Built-in bookcases with adjustable shelves work more efficiently with the owner's Longaberger baskets holding supplies.

> Work from today forward in creating a new filing system. "Don't worry about old papers. If they aren't important to you now, don't waste time on them," advises Kasey.

> Continue to check your action files and clean them out as you take the required action.

> Pay attention to aesthetics too. Your office needs to be a place you enjoy going to. Kasey softened this room with a rug, added task lighting, and hung artwork for color.

BEFORE

BEFORE

AFTER

AFTER

AFTER

Double Duty

Dual-purpose furniture allows you to furnish a spare bedroom so it's comfortable for overnight guests and dressed up enough to welcome business clients during the day. Look for club chairs or love seats that fold out into twin beds, ottomans that hold bedding, and armoires outfitted for a computer (see page 189 for sources). A wicker filing unit also serves as a nightstand.

- -

>>READER TIP

I bought an all-in-one office machine and scan the bills and receipts I want to keep to a CD. I then shred the paper. I can see a 95-percent reduction in the contents of my file drawer!

Valerie Ferrara-Ryan
Willingboro, New Jersey

No Workplace Like Home

Along one wall of an office/guest room, a mixture of stock cabinetry from a home improvement center and semicustom armoires provide a variety of storage solutions. One armoire holds the computer and the other hides the television and electronic equipment. In between, a cherry work surface rests on a stock cabinet and a towel-cubby unit that's perfect for holding rolled drawings or floor plans. A desk should be at least 30 inches wide (side to side) so you'll have enough room for working. Under the wall-hung cabinet, a pull-down message center designed for kitchen cabinets keeps a notepad and pens within reach.

How long should I keep ...

Tax records: Keep copies of returns forever. If the Internal Revenue Service claims you didn't file a return or that you filed a fraudulent return, you need forms to refute the claim: Hold onto supporting records—income, expenses, credits, and deductions, for example—for a minimum of four years. The IRS has three years to audit your return (unless it claims fraud or nonreporting, for which there is no time limit); the state has an additional year.

If you understate your gross income by 25 percent or more, the IRS has six years to audit you. Filing an amended return reopens the file for that year, so you'd need to keep those records another four years.

Keep records for property, home improvements, and investment purchases for at least three years after you sell them. Tax-related information on property you've given or received as a gift should be kept indefinitely.

Cancelled checks: These are becoming obsolete; banks save money by storing copies of cancelled checks (for 6³/₄ years) rather than returning them to you. To save even more money, some banks do paperless transactions. If you're still receiving your cancelled checks, or if you have boxes full of statements and cancelled checks because you were afraid to throw

Custom Cabinetry

For an entertainment center that needs to fit into tight quarters, look for an armoire with pocket doors that slip back into the body of the piece. This semicustom model has deep drawers below the electronic equipment to store extra bedding for times when the office is used as a guest room.

> ►►**PRO TIPS:**
> Professional organizers suggest you ask yourself these questions about every item in the room.
>
> **1. Do I use it?**
> **If yes:** When did I use it last? (If the answer is more than a year ago, you probably don't need it. Move on to the "If no" question.)
>
> **If no:** Why am I keeping it? "Because I might need it" isn't an acceptable answer! If you've had it a long time and you haven't used it, get rid of it. You obviously don't need it. If you need it in the future (9 times out of 10 you won't), there's probably a better, more effective option available.
>
> **2. How do I use it?** Make sure it's near the area where you need it and stored in a way that's conducive to its use.
>
> **3. What other items do I use it with?** Store like items together and keep things used for the same task in the same spot.
>
> "These three questions should help get you through the arduous task of clearing out the clutter," says organizing consultant Kellie Kramer. "Remember to take breaks to keep yourself fresh, reward yourself every so often for doing such hard work, and be vicious. Every little thing in the room stands between you and the end goal. Tame it or kick it out!"

them away, get out the shredder. The only reason to keep cancelled checks is in case you need proof of payment (for a service or an item) or to support a tax deduction. All other checks, ATM receipts, and deposit slips can be shredded after you balance your checkbook. Keep each bank statement until the new one arrives so you can balance your checkbook, then shred the statement. (If all checks haven't cleared, keep the statement until they do. Also retain the statements if you need to track automatic deductions.)

Utility bills and phone bills: If you deduct utility bills and telephone bills as home office expenses, keep the receipts to support your tax records. Otherwise, there's no need to keep the receipt after paying the bill, except to check the figures for consistency and accuracy. Then shred the old receipt. If you need to review your monthly bills (to track expenses or tell a prospective buyer what the utilities cost at your home), call the utility company and ask for a printout of the monthly charges for the previous two years.

Paycheck stubs or copies of direct-deposit statements: It may be useful to keep these for the tax year if you need to track deductions for health insurance, 401(k) plans, or other benefits. Otherwise retain your most recent statement as proof of employment if you apply for a loan, but shred older statements.

>>READER TIP

I use a plastic over-the-door shoe organizer to sort and store my home office supplies. The pockets are great for pens, glue, stapler and staples, scissors, CDs, and paper clips. And because it's hanging on the door, my 3-year-old child can't reach the things she shouldn't have.

Shelley D. Bowen
Hermitage, Tennessee

Credit card bills and receipts: Check receipts against the bill and then shred the receipts unless you need them to support tax deductions, warranties, or insurance claims. Check each new bill for accuracy against the previous month's bill, then shred the old one. If, however, you have had disputes with a bank or credit card company over bills, keep those records and correspondence relating to the dispute. In addition, if you often charge items with deferred billing, it's easy to get confused about whether you've been billed properly. Keeping the credit card statements for three or four months allows you to review your billing history to make sure it's correct.

Mortgage information, records for sale or purchase of a home: You'll need this information for tax purposes, so file it for at least four years (see page 125).

Records for the sale or purchase of an automobile: Keep records that will affect your taxes; see page 125.

Medical records: If you take a tax deduction for medical expenses, keep the supporting paperwork with your tax return for at least four years. It is a good idea to hold onto the explanation of benefits forms even longer. Sometimes insurance billing and payment take a long time to work their way through the system and it's possible to be billed for covered services. If you have the explanation of benefits, you can dispute the charge.

Insurance policies and bills (life, health, auto, renter's, and homeowner's): Keep the current policy and bills. There's no need to keep cancelled policies and old statements pertaining to them.

Investment records: Keep paperwork that records your initial purchase of mutual funds, stocks, bonds, and other investments; also keep the latest transaction report and year-end reports. When you sell shares, you'll need to know the purchase price and the amount of reinvested dividends and capital gains or losses to calculate your tax bill.

Adapt to Order

When you're designing storage for your home office, think outside the office box. A cosmetics sorter with sliding bins tucks into a drawer (above) to keep paint tubes and markers neatly arranged. A grid of cubbyholes (left) is usually installed in a bathroom to hold rolled-up towels, but it works equally well for floor plans or architect's drawings. When you're positioning file drawers, remember individual needs. Right-handed people need drawers on the right, but left-handed people reach for them on the left.

Customized for Comfort

In this well-designed home office/bedroom, the daybed snuggles between two multifunctional cabinets. Designed as upper cabinets, they've been customized with toe-kicks to sit on the floor. The cabinets have shallow display shelves behind multipane glass doors, but one incorporates additional deep shelves accessed from the side to maximize storage. The daybed also hides a trundle bed.

MatsonLines

HAWAII

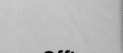

Corner Office

Slice out a little space in the living room to pay bills or tend to correspondence by choosing hardworking furniture that looks dressy enough for company. A sofa-height table serves as a desk, and the lamps shed light for reading as well as office work. The chest on a stand opens to reveal an office-in-a-box. Shop import stores and mail-order catalogs for similar items (see resources on page 189). Storage ottomans also can keep office supplies and folders handy but out of sight.

(see resources on page 189)

>>**READER TIP**

To keep my desk clear and to organize the assorted papers I want to share with close friends and family, I keep large envelopes addressed to each person. As I come across articles, recipes, cartoons, tips, coupons, photographs, and other items that will interest them, I put these in the appropriate envelopes. When the packet has enough items in it, I mail it with a short note. My 90-year-old mom especially appreciates the crossword puzzles (with solutions taped on the back), photos of the family, and easy recipes that fit her needs. My children enjoy the coupons, cartoons, and articles on their interests. Some are for a writer friend, often traveling, to catch him up on what he has missed. This method lets people know they are thought of frequently, saves time, and requires only a short note attached.

Judith Klinger
South Salem, New York

Help me find my office! To be fair, this home office also served as the temporary catchall for clutter that migrated from upstairs when another room underwent decluttering. Nevertheless, this avid collector of information piled magazines all over the room, filling the file cabinets and an old dresser. Inadequate filing systems, insufficient file storage, and a too-small desk also made this home office less than functional.

The homeowner prefers to pile rather than file—if it goes in a drawer, it's out of sight, out of mind. She needs her stacks. To help her bring order to the situation, professional organizer Shirley Stoutner suggested replacing the two-drawer file cabinets with one larger, better constructed cabinet to hold reference files (not shown). She also encouraged her to buy a desk that gave her more work space as well as storage for action files.

"My rule," says Shirley, "is don't handle anything twice. If you pick it up, pitch it or keep it—and put it where you want it when you keep it." This approach applies to the initial purging process as well as the day-to-day maintenance of order. If you're not sure whether to pitch or keep, put it in a box and seal it. If you don't miss it after six months, pitch it.

Key Ideas at Work:

> For small rooms, consider an L-shape glass and metal desk, which makes good use of space and provides plenty of surface for spreading out papers. It's visually lightweight, a bonus in this owner's small room. The industrial-chic style looks high-end but came from a local discount furniture store.

> Transform a kitchen cart into a new stand for the printer, with storage space below.

> Repaint the walls and woodwork to give the room a fresh look and enhance the work environment.

> Add desk accessories in the same finish as the desk for a sleek look that emphasizes the newly uncluttered state of the room.

> Purchase a new desk lamp to focus light where it's needed for working.

BEFORE

BEFORE

AFTER

AFTER

AFTER

Under Wraps

Blend file cabinets into your decorating scheme with a little fabric magic. The slipcover (opposite and above) is a practical way to hide reference files you don't need to access regularly. A skirted desk (below) keeps files and boxes out of sight. For the "legs" of the desk, use open cupboards that can hold metal-mesh baskets or use metal or wood file cabinets. Lay a ¾-inch pine top over them and secure a fabric panel to the edges with upholstery tacks.

>>**CHEAT SHEET:**
Photocopy this list and tape it to your file cabinet as a reminder of how long to keep papers.

> **TAX RECORDS:** Copies of returns, forever. Supporting documents: at least 4 years.

> **CHECKING ACCOUNT STATEMENTS:** 1 month or until checks clear. Keep statements that support tax deductions with your tax records for the year.

> **UTILITY BILLS:** 1 month (unless you deduct for home office expenses; file with tax records).

> **PAYCHECK STUBS OR DIRECT-DEPOSIT STATEMENTS:** 1 year.

> **CREDIT CARD STATEMENTS:** 1 to 2 months or until charges are reconciled. (Keep statements that support tax deductions with your tax records.)

> **MORTGAGE INFORMATION:** For as long as you own the property, plus 4 years for tax purposes.

> **RECORDS FOR HOME IMPROVEMENTS, SALE OR PURCHASE OF PROPERTY:** 4 years after the sale of the home or property.

> **MEDICAL RECORDS:** 4 or more years.

> **INSURANCE POLICIES AND BILLS:** Keep current policies and bills; discard cancelled policies.

> **INVESTMENT RECORDS:** Keep initial purchase and year-end reports indefinitely.

> **RECEIPTS FOR PURCHASES:** 1 month, except for big-ticket items requiring proof-of-purchase for insurance.

Basket Case

Baskets that slide into built-in shelves (above) serve as collection points for everything from magazines to toys and present a clean "wall" of texture that preserves the sense of order. Stack lidded boxes to make the wide spacing of utility shelves (opposite) more functional. Sort papers into flat-bottom handled baskets if you like to carry work into another part of the house from time to time. Hang artwork in your office too—place something low to give yourself an inspiring view when you're at your desk.

KITCHENS, PANTRIES & DINING AREAS

Kitchens are highly susceptible to clutter because they often lie on the most direct path between the family entry and other parts of the house. This is where mail, book bags, and keys get dropped; where school announcements get posted; and where bills get paid. Pantries and dining rooms fall prey to clutter because that's where things end up when they have nowhere else to go. For solutions, begin by identifying the room's true function.

Kitchens are rich with opportunities to accumulate clutter. Countertops, drawers, and cabinets easily become overcrowded and disorganized. And there's the refrigerator, accumulating empty catsup bottles, old holiday candy, and plastic containers harboring unidentifiable leftovers covered with gray sweaters of mold.

In fact, the refrigerator is a good place to start decluttering. Set aside about an hour to tackle this job, longer if your refrigerator is full. Take everything out so you can wash the shelves, door compartments, and vegetable crisper drawers. Use warm water and mild dishwashing liquid to remove spills or food particles. Rinse and dry each surface well.

Sort through the containers in the refrigerator. An overfilled refrigerator won't stay cold enough to keep food safe, so cleaning it out not only lifts your clutter-induced burden of stress but also improves the performance of your refrigerator. Throw out anything that is past its expiration date, leftovers you can't identify, and items you bought but no one likes.

In fact, leftovers you've had for more than two days probably should be tossed. As you return the remaining items to the shelves, put taller items and the ingredients you use least often at the back and keep the shorter boxes, jars, and cartons at the front where you can see them. Repeat this procedure for the freezer, then pat yourself on the back for a job well done.

Depending on the size of your kitchen and the severity of the clutter, you may be able to clean and organize the cabinets and drawers in a day. If that's overwhelming, tackle one drawer or cupboard at a time. Take out everything, sorting into four piles: "keep in this drawer or cupboard," "keep somewhere else," "give it away," and "throw it away."

Built-In Bake Center

Equipment and ingredients stay together on slide-out shelves that emerge from the recesses of the cabinet when you pull on the door (above). In the adjacent cabinet (opposite), glide-out shelves serve as pantry storage. Each shelf pulls out separately so there are no dark corners where spices can hide. On the countertop, the toaster and coffeemaker tuck into an appliance garage with its own electrical outlet.

To decide whether something should go back into the drawer, ask yourself, "When did I use this last?" If you use it regularly and that location is logically related to where you use it, put it back in the newly cleaned drawer or cabinet. If you use it often but not at that location, find a home closer to where you use it. If you haven't used it in a year, you probably don't need it; put it in one of the other piles, depending on its condition. The exceptions to this include serving platters, trays, punch bowls, or baking equipment that you use only at holiday time or for other special occasions. Keep those items in the highest cupboards since you don't need them often.

Throw out anything broken, unless you will take it to be repaired in a day or two. If you saved it thinking it would be useable if you fixed it—but you haven't—let it go. If you find two or three of something that you need only one of—timers, for instance—give one away. Consign the ratty dishcloths and towels to the ragbag and throw away stained, burned, and torn oven mitts. They're probably not doing you much good in that condition.

Do you like to have the coffeemaker, toaster oven, mugs, and cooking utensils on the counter within easy reach? Or do you prefer bare countertops? For convenience you may want to keep small appliances that you use daily on the counter. But for those you use weekly or less often, an appliance garage keeps them out of sight until you need them.

Must-Have Features

If you're planning a kitchen makeover, include a three-tier spice rack that pulls out of the cabinet next to your food preparation area (opposite). Baskets on pullout shelves store potatoes and onions (left), but could also hold linens. The pullout feature makes the contents easily accessible. The curved end of the island (below) provides a few more inches of space for jars and lunch box supplies.

▶▶READER TIP

I used to clip recipes from newspapers and magazines, but then I could never find the recipe when I was ready to make it. So I purchased a cookbook program for my computer and typed in all of the recipes. Now whenever I want to make one of them, I go to the computer and print it out. It took a bit of time but not only did it reduce my clutter, it also organized my recipes. Another plus is that the program I have allows me to search quite a few different ways, such as by ingredient; so if I have leftover buttermilk, I can search and find all the recipes that use buttermilk.

Carolyn Connerton
Rockaway, New Jersey

Storage Where You Need It

This island cooktop (right) has a downdraft vent that's hidden when not in use; under the cooktop, dividers keep pot lids separate and pans within easy reach. Wide pullout shelves with shallow baskets (below) store fruits and vegetables and could just as easily hold stacked dishware or pots and pans. If the best spot for your pullout pantry is beside the refrigerator, consider paneling the front to match the refrigerator—here, stainless steel (bottom).

Sometimes multitasking makes a mess. This kitchen isn't just where the owner prepares meals; the corner desk is a mini home office and the laundry room doubles as pantry and kitchen storage.

Working with professional organizer Kasey Vejar of Shawnee Mission, Kansas, the homeowner began by clearing the cabinets of expired foods, old spices, and infant items (such as sippy cups and baby spoons) that her child, now school age, no longer needs. She also gave away duplicates of bakeware and serving dishes.

The island became the baking center. The baking supplies—molds, pans, mixing bowls, flour, and sugar—are gathered here. Pullout baskets installed in the cabinet hold baking supplies, so the owner can see exactly what she has.

Holiday items were moved to the laundry room. The freed-up kitchen cabinets now hold all the food. Kasey advises transferring cereal from boxes into clear stackable containers because they use space more efficiently and you can see when it's time to buy more.

Pot lids, which took up the bottom 4 inches of a deep drawer, wasted valuable space. Kasey installed a pullout rack to hold the lids. She also moved the spices to the drawers beside the oven. "If you have drawer space, that's the most convenient, easy, and efficient place to keep spices," she says.

Key Ideas at Work:

➤ Clear the counters of everything you don't use daily. This makes the kitchen look much cleaner—and it makes you think twice about creating clutter.

➤ Move the food into the kitchen. Store plasticware, cups, mugs, and items related to outdoor grilling in the laundry room/pantry with other seasonal items.

➤ Make the most of cabinet space by installing vinyl-coated wire baskets or plastic bins on slide-out tracks (look for these at home improvement centers and organizing stores).

➤ Organize the desk area with baskets and small containers to sort stationery, paper clips, pens, and other office supplies. Use a mail sorter to keep track of bills, flyers, and outgoing paperwork.

➤ Dedicate one cabinet to items used daily, such as vitamins, snacks, and water bottles. Put kids' supplies at a level they can reach.

BEFORE

BEFORE

AFTER

AFTER

MINTS & GUM

ADDRESS LABELS

KEYS

MATCHES

AFTER

AFTER

BEFORE
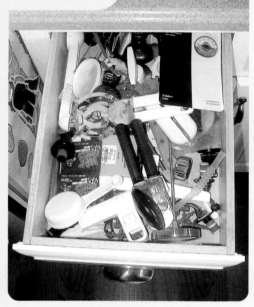

AFTER

BEFORE

Key Ideas at Work:

▶ Store items close to where they're used. Canned goods belong in the kitchen, spices beside the cooktop (not above it, where heat damages them).

▶ Separate everyday laundry supplies from those used only occasionally and from extra supplies. Several people do laundry in this household, so rounding up detergents and softeners in a basket makes it easy for them.

▶ Label containers that are not see-through so you know what's stored in each, making it easy to return things to their proper place.

AFTER

Writing on the Walls

Eliminate paper clutter in the kitchen—grocery lists, notes about upcoming meetings and events, and reminders for family members—with chalkboard walls. It's as easy as applying a coat of paint. Prime the walls, as for any paint job, then roll on blackboard paint (for sources, see page 190). Mask off a 3-inch border above the counter and below the cabinets and paint these areas with high-gloss washable paint. If food splatters onto the blackboard surface, wipe it off immediately with warm water and mild soap, rubbing very gently, and wipe dry.

Artichokes
Lemons
Butter
Onions
Potatoes
Parmigiano

If you don't have much cabinet storage, invest in a small cabinet on wheels. Inexpensive, ready-to-assemble models provide storage space in the lower cabinet and shelves for storing appliances and cookbooks above. Or adapt an antique cupboard or pantry for the purpose.

Throw out herbs or ground spices that are more than a year old; after a year, they've lost their potency and flavor. If you can't remember how long you've had an herb, give it the sniff test; if it has a strong fragrance, it still should be flavorful. Whole spices should last two years. To test them for freshness, crush or break them to release their characteristic fragrance. Don't store herbs and spices above the oven. The heat will cause them to lose flavor faster. Save time hunting for spices by organizing them alphabetically on a double-decker turntable or spice stairs.

Studies show that nearly half of the cabinet space in a kitchen is not used. The dead air between items on one shelf and the shelf above, the hard-to-reach recesses of corner cabinets, and the space under the sink present opportunities to store more and store better. Bed and bath stores offer a variety of plastic-coated wire racks and sturdy plastic "shelf helpers" and space stretchers that fit into cabinetry. Pullout features—drawers for pans and dishes, spice racks, and small-appliance drawers—come in semicustom and custom cabinets, giving you easy access to everything in the cabinet. You can retrofit your cabinets for similar functionality with vinyl-coated wire versions of pullout bins and baskets; the sliding track screws into the bottom of your cabinet. Slide-out trash can holders also are available. Check stores that specialize in organizing solutions for the home.

As you clean out cabinets, think about where you store canned goods, spices, dinnerware, glasses, and pots and pans. Are items close to where you use them? Or are you wasting time and energy walking back and forth between cabinets and preparation centers because items aren't conveniently placed? Reorganize now.

Store rice, beans, flour, cornmeal, cereal, and dry staples in square clear plastic containers with airtight lids. The

>>READER TIPS

I store rolls of waxed paper and aluminum foil standing up in a large empty coffee can that sits on the floor of my pantry. To make better use of cabinets, I installed stemmed-glass racks and cup hooks on the underside of shelves. That leaves room for smaller things below.

Sara Thomas
Bonita, California

Play beat the clock: Set a timer for 15 minutes and start putting away items in one room. When the timer rings, you're done and can move on to your next project. Do this each day and you're caught up before you know it. Fifteen minutes is a long time when you're focused on a single task.

Barbara Parish
Roy, Utah

Floating Island

Keep recipes and cookbooks in one place with a three-tier kitchen cart. Add casters so you can roll the cart over to your food prep area when you need to follow a recipe. To add casters, check the cart's stability and read the caster packaging to make sure the wheels can bear the cart's weight. Store recipes in galvanized tin boxes or galvanized lunch boxes (opposite).

Tomato Basil Bisque
4 servings

In a food processor or blender, combine
3 cups of peeled and chopped tomatoes,
a cup of chicken broth, and
8 ounces of canned tomato
Cover and blend until sm...
Stir in 2 tablespoons of c...
Cover an...

Roast Potatoes

Under the Table

Even a tiny table (left) adds work space to the kitchen. Increase its storage capacity by attaching a basket on sliding tracks to the underside of the table. (Look for baskets on sliding tracks at home improvement stores and organizing stores.) Under the farm table (opposite), an antique trunk provides convenient storage for holiday linens, party goods, and bakeware that you only use seasonally.

containers protect food from pests, make more efficient use of space, and let you see when it's time to replenish your supplies.

Keep cleaning supplies out of the reach of small children. If you store bleach and other household cleaners under the sink, put a childproof safety latch on the door. To make better use of undercounter space, check bed and bath stores for plastic and metal two-shelf systems that fit around plumbing. It's also a good idea to keep related cleaning supplies in a plastic caddy so you can take everything you need from room to room.

It's wise to keep a small fire extinguisher in the kitchen and garage. Check the gauge once a year to make sure it's still charged. If the needle slips into the red zone, have the extinguisher recharged. Check in the Yellow Pages under "Fire Extinguishers." It may cost about $18 to recharge a 5-pound extinguisher.

If the kitchen counter is the dumping ground for mail, backpacks, books, and keys, carve out spaces to handle these functions and leave the kitchen counter clean and clutter-free. Create a mini office for the mail and related supplies—a letter sorter, napkin holder, or old-fashioned toast server can hold the mail. Insert dividers in the drawer and use them to store pens, pencils, scissors, adhesive tape, a letter opener, and stamps. To handle the backpacks and books, reorganize the area beside your entry: Add pegs and wall-mounted cubes inside the door to give kids an alternative place to put their stuff.

>>**READER TIP**

I save empty facial tissue boxes and stuff all my plastic grocery bags in them. They hold a lot, keeping the bags tidy in a very small amount of storage space. I grab a full box when I go camping. I store another under the kitchen sink. I refill it when I come home from grocery shopping and use the bags all week.

Elvira Mitchell
Goodyear, Arizona

This pantry was trying to serve too many purposes. Decorating items, small appliances, and glassware as well as household staples took up valuable space. In addition, food items weren't logically organized, so it was hard to tell when supplies were low.

"Our goal was for this to be the main holding space for food," says professional organizer Kasey Vejar of Shawnee Mission, Kansas. "I like to set up a pantry like a grocery store." Baking items are grouped together, as are canned soups, vegetables, and dry cereals.

The small appliances—woks and blenders, for example—were moved to the lower level. "You don't want to reach over your head to pull down heavy items," cautions Kasey.

The homeowner likes the look of wicker, so Kasey used fabric-lined wicker baskets to organize snacks and keep them neatly confined. Grouping similar items in containers helps ensure that you don't buy more than you can conveniently use. Label every container so anyone (including visitors) can find things easily.

To make better use of "dead space" between shelves, Kasey used a combination of under-the-shelf baskets, vinyl-coated wire shelf helpers, and heavy-duty plastic stair-step expanders that guarantee items won't get lost at the back of the pantry. They also allow the owner to check inventory at a glance.

Key Ideas at Work:

➤ Clear out expired foods and spices and purge the collection of plastic containers. Keep only a few containers for leftovers. Use clear plastic containers with airtight lids to store dry cereals, baking supplies, and pet food. Label everything.

➤ Use stair-step shelf expanders to store canned goods and bottled items. Group items as you would find them in a grocery store, organized by type.

➤ Add under-the-shelf baskets to hold boxed snacks or napkins and place mats for everyday use.

➤ Group condiments, sauces, and other liquids on a plastic turntable. It makes good use of corner space, spins for easy access, and is easy to clean up in case of drips.

➤ Use vinyl-coated wire shelf helpers to stack pot lids and cookie sheets and to create an extra storage surface between shelves.

BEFORE

AFTER

Creative Storage

Repurposed flea market finds give character to kitchen storage. Use an old tool caddy to hold utensils and cooking supplies (below), a vintage set of drawers from a machine shop to store flatware and napkins (opposite), and metal flowerpots to hold utensils. Wide-mouth vessels serving as cookware caddies let you pull out one piece at a time—easier to deal with than a drawer full of jumbled tools. Store table linens, dish towels, and aprons in labeled baskets.

Orderly bliss comes to the pantry. This pantry held the cook's library, assorted food supplies and serving trays, and pet food. Mops, brooms, and a stepladder leaning against the wall made it tough to get to anything on the shelves.

The first step to cleaning involved relocating mops, brooms, and the stepladder to the laundry room and hanging them on hooks to keep the floor clear.

Remember to save the "prime real estate" (eye-level shelves) for items you use often. Bulk items that you don't need every day, such as extra paper towels and garbage bags, can go in baskets for storage on the top shelf.

Collecting similar items into baskets helps clean up the chaotic look of miscellaneous jars and cans jostling for space on the shelves. The baskets also present a united front that greets the owner's eye with a tidier appearance when she opens the pantry door.

Transferring grains, rice, and cereals to clear plastic or glass canisters provides airtight storage and lets the owner see when it's time to replenish stock. Investing in a $20 label maker to mark each container eliminates confusion about contents.

Line wicker baskets with paper towels or fabric to store onions. This keeps the skins from filtering through.

Key Ideas at Work:

➤ Use wicker baskets lined with fabric to store dish towels and linens, boxed crackers, bottled drinks, and bags of pasta. Baskets at floor level can hold newspapers and bottles for recycling.

➤ Get rid of unsightly opened bags of pet food and make better use of storage space by transferring the dry pet food into a large flip-top plastic container that fits under the bottom shelf of the pantry.

➤ Hang an inexpensive plate rack on the wall to store serving platters.

➤ Put the back of the pantry door to work by hanging a wall rack. Store oils, vinegars, and seasonings there along with other frequently used items.

➤ Tuck a small footstool under the bottom shelf to make it easy to reach the top shelf.

BEFORE

BEFORE

CASE STUDY: PANTRY

Key Ideas at Work:

> Create a wine rack from inexpensive wooden wine boxes from a home and linens store. Spray-paint them inside and out and stack on one side of the pantry. Use this area to store bottled water as well as wine.

> Hang an erasable board in the pantry to jot down items that need replenishing.

> Keep candles and lighter together in a basket so they're handy when you're entertaining.

AFTER

AFTER

AFTER

AFTER

AFTER

BALSAMIC VINEGAR
RAISINS
ORZO
BUTTER
RED PEPPERS

Fresh and Fun

Refreshing color on walls, floor, and seating induces an uncluttered state of mind. Storage tailored to the room's principal function—small gatherings that focus on wine-tasting—keeps essential supplies in their proper place. The wine rack and table are built from Baltic birch plywood and galvanized pipe.

Dining Areas

If your dining room is a dumping ground for papers, books, boxes, and bikes, maybe you don't need a dining room. Maybe what you really need is a home office, hobby room, or storage room. In that case, sell the dining table and chairs and furnish the room to suit your needs.

If, on the other hand, you like to have sit-down meals from time to time, a compromise may be in order. Move the table to one side and convert the remaining wall space or corners to storage and desk space. When you want to seat people around the table, pull it away from the wall.

Office supply stores sell armoires outfitted as mini offices. When you have a party, close the doors, and no one will be the wiser. Or use a buffet, sideboard, or even a dresser to store office or hobby supplies along with table linens, china, and glassware.

For a quick do-it-yourself worktable-desk in the dining room, lay a hollow-core door on a pair of filing cabinets. Standard doors are 24×80 inches. Paint the door to match your walls and skirt it with fabric (simply staple the long folded edge of the fabric to the edge of the door, then glue ribbon trim over the staples). The skirt will hide the file cabinets and anything else you tuck under the desk, giving you out-of-sight storage space and the room a finished look. The table can double as a buffet server when you entertain.

A wall of bookshelves in the dining room creates an intimate dining-in-the-library feeling and provides space to store files, paperwork, and hobby supplies. Sort through your stuff and store it in lidded boxes or deep, rectangular baskets so the shelves look tidy and attractive. Label the containers so you can find what you need at a glance.

>>READER TIPS

I have a few sets of measuring cups, and I put them right into my flour, sugar, powdered sugar, oatmeal, etc. That way when I start to bake, I don't have to look for them; they're right at hand.

Jill Snyder
Koshkonong, Missouri

I store all my baking supplies in a plastic storage cart with drawers. The small drawers hold icing tips and pastry bags, and the large drawers hold specialty pans and cookie cutters. When I'm ready to bake, I just wheel the cart over to my island.

Shelley D. Bowen
Hermitage, Tennessee

Hide the Clutter

If your dining room doubles as a study area, play space, or work space, these curtained shelves offer an ideal way to store books and toys quickly when it's time to set the table. Make the panels from plain cotton canvas. Hem the bottom and side edges and stitch a rod pocket along the top edge to receive a tension rod. Use lower compartments for things the kids need and reserve the higher shelves for items you don't want little hands to reach. Display books or a few bold accessories on the uncurtained shelves.

Small space, big clutter. A small kitchen meant storage spilled over into the dining room in this apartment. The owners entertain regularly and tried to solve the storage problem with chests, cabinets, and shelves. Over time, however, items accumulated on the floor and on top of the furniture.

Professional organizer Barbara Brock of New York City helped sort items into entertaining and everyday uses. An antique bombé chest stores linens, candles, and special-occasion items.

To handle everything else, Barbara installed 14- and 18-inch-deep adjustable shelves in the dining room's 30-inch-deep niche. Enclosing the niche completely would make the room feel too cramped, but the narrow, floor-to-ceiling shelves allow the room to retain a formal look while providing plenty of storage. The system she used has a horizontal metal track that attaches to the wall. Sides with predrilled holes hang on the track and are held in place by the top and bottom shelves.

Barbara divided the shelves into sections for bar accessories; china, glassware, and accessories for entertaining; and everyday items. Labeling the shelves helps everyone know where things go.

To keep the dining area light and airy, Barbara concealed the shelves behind light-color floor-to-ceiling silk curtains. Hung on a brass rod with brass clutch rings, they're easy to make, elegant, and functional.

Key Ideas at Work:

> Maximize the room's architecture by filling a deep niche with floor-to-ceiling shelves. Shop home improvement centers or organizing stores for ready-made closet systems with adjustable shelves so you can vary the spacing depending on the items to be stored.

> Separate items according to everyday use, entertaining use, barware, and special occasion. Designate a portion of the storage space to each use. Label shelves.

> Choose shelves deep enough to accommodate dinner plates or two rows of glasses. If shelves are too deep, items will be harder to access. Follow Barbara's motto: "Easy access is easy living."

> Install simple floor-to-ceiling draperies to hide the shelves when you're not taking things out or putting things away. In closing off the busyness, the fabric helps calm the mood of the room.

BEFORE

AFTER

AFTER

AFTER

AFTER

Double-Duty Buffet

When you're serving dinner from the elegant skirted buffet (opposite), guests will never guess that you stowed your office work underneath (above). Shop home improvement centers or organizing stores for a pair of metal frame units with slide-out wire baskets. Buy a ready-made laminate or unfinished pine board to lay on top. Paint the pine to match the skirt fabric, and attach the skirt to the board using hook-and-loop tape.

Use dining room storage pieces to catch the spillover from the kitchen. This is the logical place to keep your best china and crystal, special-occasion linens, gravy boat, crystal salt and pepper shakers, platters, and punch bowls that only come out for holidays or big parties.

Decorate the cabinet shelves as you would bookcase shelves. They're part of the room's scenery, and the effect should be orderly and calming. Top a low stack of plates with a cup or goblet, alternate low horizontal pieces with tall vertical ones, and use cake platters as pedestals to show off a ring of demitasse cups or a pretty cream and sugar set.

Do-It-Yourself China Cabinet

Create cottage-style dining room storage from two unfinished bookcases. Adding swing-arm fabric doors at the base imparts the look of a real hutch. An antiqued finish and paper doilies, attached to the shelf edge with double-stick tape, suggest Swedish styling. If a cottage look isn't your style, paint or stain the bookcases in the color of your choice—for example, black bookcases with bamboo "curtain" panels for an Asian feeling, or bright red with retro fabric panels for a fun and funky look.

Help me find my dining table! Limited storage space in this 1940s home meant that papers, magazines, and notes stacked up on the dining room table. The owner's bicycle ended up in here as well. The room needed to serve as an office but also needed to be accessible for sit-down dinner parties as well as casual meals.

Working with professional organizer Monica Ricci, the homeowner began sorting through stacks of papers. Paper clutter is the most daunting clutter-buster task because you have to look at each piece and make a decision. Monica suggested the owner create separate stacks: magazines for fun, magazines for work, notes, maps, cards from friends, cancelled checks and ATM receipts, items requiring action, and items to be shredded.

To provide storage and a work surface, the owner bought a sofa table rather than a more conventional buffet or credenza. The height makes it suitable to use as a serving table, while the piece is the perfect size to fit the small proportions of the room. The drawers store the smaller paper items (maps, cards and letters, and receipts) as well as candles and lighter. Under the table a pair of deep wicker baskets hold the magazines the owner reads for pleasure and the publications and folders she needs for work.

Ottomans serve as seating and open up to provide storage for telephone directories and additional reference materials.

Key Ideas at Work:

➤ Assess the functions each room needs to serve. This owner has sit-down dinners around a handsome mahogany dining table; the room also has to serve as a work space.

➤ Bring in a multifunction storage piece scaled to fit the room. A sofa table can provide drawer space and a serving/work surface, with room underneath for additional storage.

➤ Move extraneous furniture—such as the old telephone table and chair—out of the room.

➤ Look for unexpected seating options. Storage ottomans found at a flea market were professionally reupholstered for use as dining table seating. Like the upholstered bench, they take up little space visually and can be pushed under the table to free up floor space.

BEFORE

BEFORE

AFTER

BEFORE

Key Ideas at Work:

> Banish the bicycle to the garage or storage room. Align the slipcovered parsons chairs with the wall for a squared-up, orderly look when the dining room isn't being used for entertaining.

> Use deep wicker baskets to sort reading material into "for fun" and "for work." Stash these under the sofa table where they're accessible and out of the way. Dark-color wicker blends with the wood of the sofa table for a unified look.

> Use the sofa table drawers as a mini file cabinet. See-through tinted plastic folders can hold small papers—credit card receipts, ATM receipts, and bills—and stack neatly in the drawer.

> Bring in a pair of tall, slender lamps for the sofa table to introduce mood lighting for evening gatherings.

> Store office supplies in an attractive wicker storage box on the sofa table.

AFTER

AFTER

LAUNDRY ROOMS, BASEMENTS & GARAGES

Basements, garages, and laundry rooms are the final frontier for clutter. After all, that's what those spaces are for, right? Even the areas designated for catchall storage will function much better if you apply the professional organizers' principles of sorting, letting go, and discovering new systems that work for you. Workable storage means you can find the holiday wrapping paper or your garden tools when you need them without a maddening hours-long search.

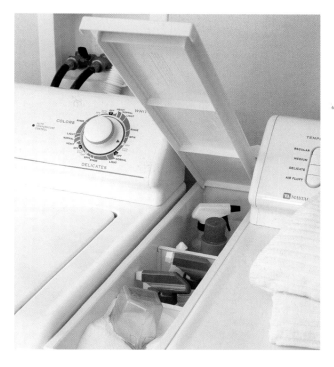

Laundry areas should be pretty easy to keep clutter-free—you don't need anything more than a washer, dryer, detergent, and maybe some dryer sheets or fabric softener. Usually the clutter culprits are those non-laundry items you don't know where else to store. This area, which is synonymous with cleanliness, should stay sparkling and pristine: no dust, no sticky detergent spills, and no fragments of facial tissue that weren't removed from a pocket before washing. Keep a sponge nearby so you can wipe up spills immediately.

Install shelves or cupboards above the washer and dryer to stash detergent, stain removers, and dryer sheets. If there's room between the cupboards, fit a sturdy tension rod between them to hang clothes as you take them out of the dryer.

The most practical location for laundry baskets is not necessarily in the laundry room but where the dirty clothes collect. Put one in the closet of each bedroom or in each bathroom. Better yet, give each person two baskets or laundry bags, one for dark clothes and one for whites and lights. That way laundry is presorted when it arrives at the washing machine.

Take clothes out of the dryer and fold or hang them right away to minimize wrinkling and to avoid the piles of unsorted, unfolded clothes.

If you don't have room to keep the ironing board set up all the time, set aside an hour on Sunday night to press the clothes you plan to wear in the coming week. You'll save time deciding what to wear every morning too.

In a space-starved apartment or house, an over-the-door ironing board can be a practical alternative to a full-size one. Keep in mind they're lightweight and best only for light touch-ups rather than serious pressing.

Good Design

In this 9×10-foot laundry room (opposite), a 3-inch-deep base raises the standard cabinet to put the counter at a more comfortable height for working while standing. Open niches receive laundry baskets for sorting, washing, or folding clothes. A rod between the upper cabinets holds clothes that need to drip-dry. Between the washer and dryer on the opposite wall, a clothes-care caddy with a lift-top lid (above) holds detergent and fabric softener.

- -

>>READER TIP

I always used to write notes, lists, and phone numbers or messages on pieces of paper, which I would sometimes lose. So I bought a memo book with carbon sheets (the kind that's often used for taking phone messages) from an office supply store. Now I write my notes and take the top sheet with me, but I always have the copy that's still in the memo book just in case.

Beatriz Seinuk-Ackerman
New York, New York

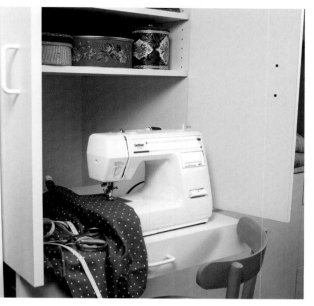

Behind Closed Doors

In planning the perfect laundry room, consider custom cabinetry designed with drop-out ironing boards (opposite) and a pullout shelf for the sewing machine (above). The ironing cupboard accommodates a full-size and a sleeve-size ironing board as well as an electrical outlet and a place for the iron. A sturdy metal rod pulls out of the adjoining cabinet to hold pressed clothes.

▶▶READER TIP

I cleaned out the storage area of my home and found sewing patterns from high school (I have been out of school for 25 years). I also discovered a stack of outdated computer handbooks. Currently I am going through all of our pictures and keeping only the ones with meaning (some I cannot even tell what it was). I organize them by year and event in photo storage boxes. In addition, all of the holiday decorations I decided to keep are in plastic bins with lids and labeled in one section of my storage area.

Diane Keller
Broadview Heights, Ohio

Clean and Pretty

If you don't have space for built-in cabinets and countertops, use a chrome utility unit (above), available through mail-order catalogs (see page 190). The solid-surface waist-high shelf provides folding space, and baskets above and below store laundry supplies. A white shelf with knobs (opposite) takes advantage of empty wall space to provide storage for supplies, an open display area, and a place to hang damp clothing. Cubbies replaced standard wire shelving (right) for a space-smart attractive look above the washer and dryer. Baskets and glass canisters store supplies with style.

CASE STUDY: BASEMENT

Make a clean sweep. Chaos didn't take over this basement, but it was more disorganized than the homeowners wanted it to be. Working with professional organizer Shari Hudson of Des Moines, Iowa, the homeowners defined the goals for the space—attractive, accessible storage and clearly identified recreational spaces.

Focus on one area at a time, says Shari, so you don't get overwhelmed. She pulled everything out from under the stairs. The homeowners went through every box and bag, sorting into "keep," "charity," and "garbage" piles. As things went into the "keep" pile, Shari divided them into like items—books, tools, household items, hobby items, games, memorabilia, photos, and holiday decorations.

When sorting holiday decorations, says Shari, store garland in one box, lights in another, and gift wrap in another. Sort miscellaneous holiday items into linens, tabletop decorations, wreaths and wall decorations, and yard decorations. The more focused your categories, the easier it will be to find exactly what you want when you need it.

Shari advises buying containers before building or buying shelving. That way you can space the shelving properly. The homeowner built his own shelves using sturdy 2×4s to fit the space under the stairs; he painted them glossy white for a crisp, graphic appearance. Cans of paint needed for touch-ups moved to another area. Storage bins, picnicware, folding chairs, and a card table now sit two deep so everything is easy to reach.

Key Ideas at Work:

> Take oil-base paint, building materials, water sealant, and unused propane to the hazardous-waste disposal site. Allow latex paint to dry out before putting it in the garbage. If latex paint cans are rusted shut, spray with penetrating oil to loosen the seal; pour paint onto newspapers to dry.

> Paint the poured-concrete walls to brighten the space. Paint the stairs and landing for a more finished look.

> Use plastic bins rather than cardboard boxes for storage. Cardboard boxes will absorb the moisture that concrete walls emit—even during winter.

> Plan shelving to accommodate the depth and height of storage containers. Avoid stacking containers so you don't have to move three bins to get at the fourth.

> Customize the choice of bins to suit the size, shape, and quantity of items to be stored.

BEFORE

BEFORE

AFTER

AFTER

AFTER

Key Ideas at Work:

➤ For a clean look, skirt the television table and hide videos and games underneath.

➤ Dedicate the metal shelving unit to gardening and home maintenance supplies. Hang as many items as possible (such as deck chairs and garden equipment) to keep the floor clear. This makes better use of wall space, and keeping the floor uncluttered makes the area look neater.

➤ Coil garden hoses inside large planters to minimize the space they take up.

➤ Add a simple white cabinet to house board games, table tennis paddles, and other recreational equipment.

➤ Decorate: The homeowner hung a bus-stop sign he made to propose to his wife 20 years ago. A garden bench underneath makes it a focal point.

AFTER

BEFORE

BEFORE

AFTER

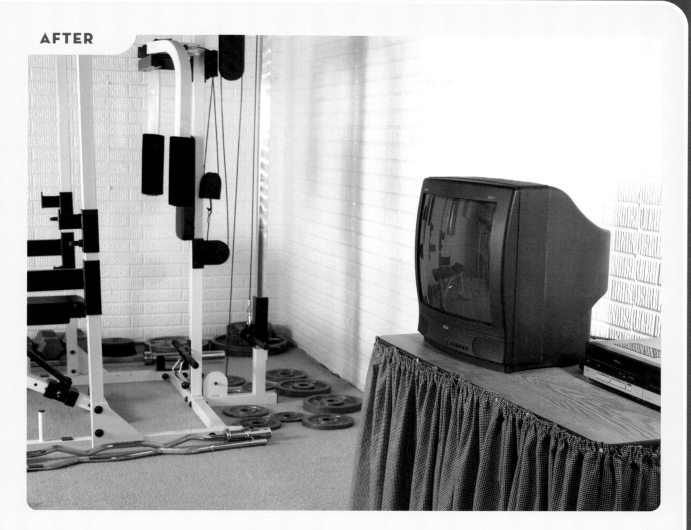

AFTER

AFTER

BASEMENTS

Basements are prime candidates for clutter because you don't spend much time down there, so the motto "out of sight, out of mind" is in full operation. But basements provide prime storage space when well planned. First look at what you need to store, then design and purchase shelving, bins, and tubs accordingly. Avoid stacking boxes or tubs on top of each other because you'll have to remove the top ones to reach the bottom one that you need. Instead, measure the height and width of the storage tubs, then build shelves from 2×4s, spacing the shelves the height of the tubs plus 1 or 2 inches for easy access. Plan for the bottom shelf to be about 4 inches above the floor so you can vacuum underneath from time to time.

Basements tend to be humid and damp, so they're not the best location for storing books, paper items, photographs, and stuffed animals, which can be ruined by mildew. Tools or cans of paint also are subject to rust in damp basements. If this is the only place you have for storage, use a dehumidifier to help dry out the air. Basements are great for storing items not affected by moisture, such as dishware, pottery, glassware, holiday ornaments and lights, artificial wreaths and trees, and plastic toys.

Laundry in a Cabinet

A cutout in the shelf (opposite) makes room for the ironing board without sacrificing an entire shelf. Turn a laminated armoire into a laundry closet (left and below). Check the door hinges to be sure they can bear the weight of the ironing board. You'll find ironing board mounting kits at home centers; you may need to screw a block of scrap wood to the top of the door to accept the square hooks. Use teak outdoor planters as laundry sorters.

▶▶READER TIP

With three active children, the stacks of paper coming home from school and other activities becomes overwhelming. Our solution was to create three-ring binders. One binder has a section for each child's school and a section for each activity (Scouts, gymnastics, etc.). Another binder contains names and addresses, including telephone directories from the neighborhood and church. It also has a section for directions to the homes of various friends. This has worked so well for us that we've started binders for copies of recipes, gardening tips, and manuals for computer software.

Beverly Taylor
Crystal Lake, Illinois

CASE STUDY: GARAGE

A place of last resort was the fate of this garage, which served as a dumping ground for everything that the owners hadn't found a spot for inside their new house. When it was time to tackle the garage, they wanted the space to store sports and garden equipment and to accommodate a workshop and fitness equipment.

The couple found that working with professional organizer Shari Hudson of Des Moines, Iowa, gave them "permission" to let go of items by forcing them to decide what they really needed. "It became apparent that we were holding onto items we didn't need, didn't want, and couldn't use," said the homeowner.

Because they were on a low budget, they opted to combine affordable shelving and racks from various sources, accomplishing the makeover for about $300.

The long blank wall opposite the garage door became the workshop area. The couple bought three 4-foot-long workbenches with top shelves to fill the wall. They mounted pegboard to hang items below the shelves. Totes, tools, and materials are organized by use: auto-related items on the left, general tools in the middle, and tools for building speakers on the right.

The couple built shelves on each side wall from extra-heavy-duty brackets and particleboard shelving cut to size at a home center. To hang bikes and garden equipment, they mounted 2×4s and inserted heavy-duty hooks.

Key Ideas at Work:

> Make the most of wall space. Shelves made from brackets and particleboard can hold items such as skis, sleeping bags, a cooler, and tubs that store home and garden supplies. Choose heavy-duty brackets and make sure they are securely attached to studs so they can bear the weight.

> Hang bikes on one wall and garden equipment on the other, using 2×4s and heavy-duty hooks. Drill holes in wooden handles (such as shovels or axes) and thread with a leather thong to make hanging easy.

> Build a workshop using ready-to-assemble workbenches. Add pegboard to the wall above to hang small tools so they're easy to find quickly. Store large or heavy items on the bottom shelf.

> Mount a plastic-coated wire rack, typically used in laundry areas, near the back door for motorcycle helmets and jackets.

BEFORE

BEFORE

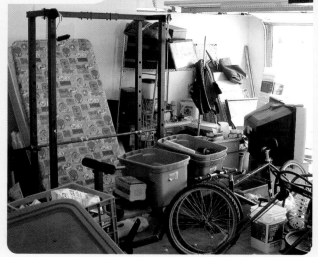

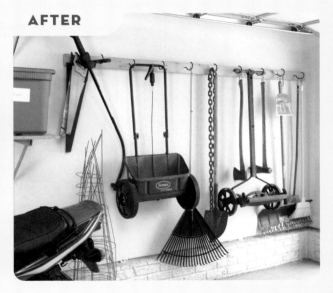

The Organized Garage

Combine modular cabinets and shelves (below) to turn one wall into an all-purpose home-and-garden storage center. If space is too tight for freestanding units, shop for wall-hung rack and shelf systems (below right and opposite). Vertical tracks are suspended from a horizontal mounting bar and shelves with brackets can be inserted at any spacing required. Wall-mounted tool holders and storage racks (opposite below) help keep floor space clear.

GARAGES

Garages often end up housing the lawn mower, yard equipment and supplies, gardening tools, and sports equipment as well as the car. In fact sometimes there's no room for the car. If this is your dilemma, you may need to buy a shed or outbuilding to store the yard equipment and gardening tools. First, however, go through the sorting and tossing process. Get rid of anything broken, give away or sell duplicates, toss anything you haven't used in a year, and then assess what you have left.

Choose a sunny, warm day (or at least a day without rain) to clean out the garage so you're not pulling everything out when it's raining or snowing. And you do want to pull everything out. It's essential to start with a clean slate to create a more organized space.

Leftover oil-base paint can last for up to 15 years if stored properly; latex paint can remain usable for up to 10 years. To keep the paint from drying out, wipe the rims of the can and lid to remove dripped paint; cover the top of the can with plastic wrap, then pound the lid in place. Some people suggest turning the can upside down, but most professional painters don't do this. Store paint in a cool, dry location; the garage is generally ideal because paint won't be exposed to extreme heat or cold there. Heat causes paint to deteriorate, so don't stack cans close to a water heater or furnace. Also protect the paint from freezing.

To dispose of old latex paint, let it dry in the can or pour it out onto newspaper and let it dry. Dispose of oil-base paints at a hazardous waste site; check your phone book for the location of a site in your area.

To determine the kind of storage solutions you'll need, group items by category or kind: sports equipment, lawn care equipment and supplies, automotive supplies, and home maintenance supplies and tools. Professional organizer Kasey Vejar of Shawnee Mission, Kansas, recommends dividing the garage into zones: gardening and lawn care, recycling, automotive, home improvement, general hardware, and sports and recreational equipment.

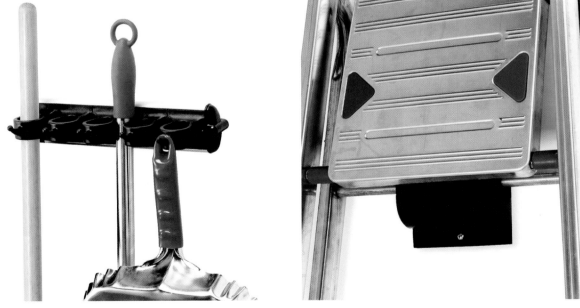

Tool Collectors

Rakes, brooms, shovels, and other home-and-garden maintenance tools are easy to access when each one stands upright rather than stacked in a corner. Heavy-duty plastic tool towers fit snugly into a corner or line up along the wall. (See page 190 for sources.)

Shop home centers, hardware stores, wholesale clubs, and sporting goods stores for storage systems geared to garages (or see page 190 for resources). Look for stain-resistant laminate or plastic finishes, stainless steel, or hardwood cabinets and shelving treated to withstand humidity and solvents.

Store hazardous chemicals—fertilizers, gasoline, oil, paint thinner, and kerosene—in locked cabinets out of the reach of children. Within the cabinets, continue to group items by function: fertilizers and pesticides, paint and solvents, and oil and gas.

Put wall space to work. Wall organizational systems with panels that support shelves, hooks, and cabinets offer the ultimate in flexibility and uniform good looks but can be a big investment. For more affordable options, look for wall-hanging systems that offer a variety of component parts, such as bike racks, garden-hose hooks, wire baskets, bins, and movable shelves. You can customize these systems to serve as garden storage, automotive equipment centers, or storage for sports equipment.

Create wall systems with shelf brackets, 2×4s, and heavy-duty hooks (see page 183). To keep garden tools off the floor and out of the way (and within easy reach): Nail a 2×4 along one wall just above head height and hammer pairs of nails along the length, spacing them so each pair can support the head of a rake, hoe, or shovel.

Use overhead space as well. Check home improvement stores for ceiling-mounted shelves that take advantage of otherwise wasted space. The units are adjustable so they can even go above the open garage door (see page 190 for more information).

Hang bikes on bike-rack hooks. Install shelf brackets to hang ladders horizontally or to hang folded lawn chairs.

Look Up for Storage

Take advantage of ceiling space in the garage with an easy-to-install ceiling-mounted shelving system (see page 190 for sources). The down rod can be adjusted from 16 inches to 28 inches, so the shelves will clear a garage door.

RESOURCES

National Association of Professional Organizers:

To find a member near you, visit www.napo.net

Professional Organizers Who Contributed to This Book:

Barbara Brock, closet designer/organizer, and Kathleen Ong, professional organizer, A Proper Place, New York, New York; 212/755-1017; aproperplace.com; email: bbrock@nyc.rr.com

Shari Hudson
Organized by Design
954 Glen Oaks Terrace
West Des Moines, IA 50266
Shudson@organizedbydesign.net
organizedbydesign.net

Monica Ricci
Catalyst Organizing Solutions
Phone: 770/569-2642
Fax: 770/569-2641
monica@catalystorganizing.com
catalystorganizing.com

Shirley Stoutner
Remarkable Order
515/210-8735
shirley@remarkableorder.com
remarkableorder.com

Kasey Vejar
Simply Organized, Inc.
P.O. Box 12652
Shawnee Mission, KS 66282
913/269-5920
kasey@kcorganizers.com
kcorganizers.com

Entries:

Page 12: galvanized magazine rack; 85-1115-88, Pottery Barn; 800/922-5507; potterybarn.com

Family Rooms:

Pages 28–29: cube modular units: Sauder; 800/523-3987; sauder.com. Pillow: Crate & Barrel; 800/323-5461; crateandbarrel.com

Pages 30–31: cube modular units: Sauder; 800/523-3987; sauder.com

Page 32: magazine files: IKEA Home Furnishings; 800/434-4532. Chair: Mitchell Gold; for a retailer call 800/789-5401; mitchellgold.com

Page 34 bottom: cube modular units: Sauder; 800/523-3987; sauder.com

Bedrooms:

Pages 46–47: Closet construction: James F. Lutes, Inc., Construction, 1071 Guizot St., San Diego, CA 92107; 619/225-0822. Mirrors: MSG, 4360 Morena Blvd., San Diego, CA 92117; 858/274-5277

Page 50: custom lingerie chest, custom TV insert: Pete's Cabinets, 1303 E. Casino Rd., Everett, WA 98203; 425/745-1053

Pages 52–53: lamp: IKEA Home Furnishings; 800/434-4532. Modular shelves, picture frames, white quilt, shoes: Target Stores; 800/800-8800; target.com

Pages 62–63: étagère, folding mesh cubes, stow-away containers: The Container Store: 800/733-3532; containerstore.com. Picnic table: Crate & Barrel; 800/323-5461; crateandbarrel.com

Pages 64–65: trundle bed with storage, nightstand: Stanley Furniture; 276/627-2200; stanleyfurniture.com

Closets:

Page 75: Trademark Custom Woodwork, 11675 Sorrento Valley Rd., Suite M, San Diego, CA 92121; 858/792-5363

RESOURCES

Pages 80–83: Design by Kasey Vejar, Simply Organized, Inc., Shawnee Mission, Kansas. Carpentry and assembly, Larry Welch; organizing assistant, Billy Welch; contact through Simply Organized, Inc. Shelves/cabinetry: Lowe's; lowes.com. Floral storage boxes: Hobby Lobby; hobbylobby.com. Pink storage boxes, plastic purse chain: Organized Living; organizedliving.com. Pale blue bins, white plastic hangers, skirt hangers: Target. Black and silver storage boxes: Tuesday Morning; tuesdaymorning.com

Pages 88–89: Design by Barbara Brock, A Proper Place, New York, New York. Cream utility totes (holding lightbulbs, candles, materials); expandable cutlery tray for hardware, hammer, screwdrivers, pliers; mesh wire file bin for wrapping paper: Bed Bath & Beyond; bedbathandbeyond.com. Mesh wire bins with handles (holding paints, cleaning cloths), white cardboard carton (holding sponges, cleaning supplies), white grid wall panel, white Akrobin (long small, narrow medium, wide medium); Elfa frame and white top: The Container Store; containerstore.com

Home Offices:

Pages 106–107: armoire, "Palace," Urban Evolutions; 888/695-7893; urbanevolutions.com

Page 109: Design by Kasey Vejar, Simply Organized, Inc., Shawnee Mission, Kansas. Carpentry and assembly, Larry Welch; organizing assistant, Billy Welch; contact through Simply Organized, Inc. Furniture and accessories: Organized Living; organizedliving.com. Baskets on shelves: Longaberger Baskets; longaberger.com

Pages 110–111: Sleeper chairs, 73015, 6040-32; ottoman, 73011, 6040-32: Action Ind., The Lane Co. Computer armoire, 6640-295 (Espresso): Sauder; 800/523-3987; sauder.com. Shutters on closet doors: Smith + Noble; for a catalog, call 800/765-7776.

Pages 112–119: interior designer: Patricia Gaylor, Patricia Gaylor Interiors, 265 Longhill Rd., Little Falls, NJ 07424; 973/746-2092. Maple cabinetry and organization systems: Merillat Industries, P.O. Box 1946, Adrian, MI 49221; 800/575-8763; merillat.com; see Organomics on website. Furniture: Maine Cottage, P.O. Box 935, Yarmouth, ME 04096; 207/846-1430; mainecottage.com. Bedding and solid color pillows: Ann Gish. Accessories: Pottery Barn; potterybarn.com

Pages 120–121: colonial wood desk and chair: Palacek; 800/274-7730; palacek.com. Wooden chest: Pier 1 Imports, 800/245-4595; pier1.com

Kitchens:

Pages 130–131: kitchen designer: Dawn Sullivan, Allied Member, ASID, DAS Interiors. General contractor: Johansen Construction and Tile; 760/741-6834. Custom cabinets, DAS Interiors

Pages 132–133: kitchen designer, Lesa Heebner. Cabinets: Finest City Cabinets, 330-A Trousdale Dr., Chula Vista, CA 91910; 619/585-0202. Cabinet hardware, oiled bronze, Detail, 503 N. La Cienega Blvd., W. Hollywood, CA 90069; 310/659-1550

Pages 134–135: Cabinets: David Brothers Cabinetmakers, Escondido, CA. Cooktop, GE Appliances, GE Answer Center; 800/626-2000. Vent: Dacor, 1440 Bridge Gate Dr., Diamond Bar, CA 91765; 800/793-0093. (Page 134 bottom): kitchen design, Shirley McFarlane, CKD, 800 Miami Circle, Suite 100, Atlanta, GA 30324; 404/262-1547. Stainless-steel panels: Heritage Custom Kitchens, Inc., 215 Diller Ave., New Holland, PA 17557; 717/351-1700.

Pages 136–139: Design by Kasey Vejar, Simply Organized, Inc., Shawnee Mission, Kansas. Pull-out wire bin and white plastic baskets, page 138, Organized Living; canisters: Kmart. Wicker baskets in laundry cabinet page 139: Dollar General. Green tins: Pottery Barn Kids. Large glass jars: Martha

RESOURCES

Stewart/Kmart. Additional accessories: Target, Kmart, Dollar General, Bed Bath & Beyond. Baskets: Longaberger Baskets; 740/321-3447; longaberger.com

Pages 140–141: chalkboard paint: Crayola Paint; purchase at crafts or hardware stores; high gloss trim: 825 Blue, Benjamin Moore; for dealer call 800/826-2623

Page 142: wicker cart (casters added): Pier 1, 800/447-4371; pier1.com

Pages 146–147: Design by Kasey Vejar, Simply Organized, Inc., Shawnee Mission, Kansas. Expand-A-Shelf stair-step shelves available in small, medium, and large from several online sources; search under ExpandAShelf. Organized Living sells the medium size; visit organizedliving.com. Target and Wal-mart sell the small size (suitable for spices). For vinyl-coated wire racks, mini-shelves, and under-the-shelf baskets with or without sliding tracks: Organized Living, organizedliving.com; Bed Bath & Beyond, bedbathandbeyond.com; or Target, target.com

Page 156: horizontal shelves: Hold Everything; for a catalog call 800/421-2264. Tension rods for canvas fabric panels: Kirsch; for a catalog or a retailer near you call 800/528-1407

Pages 158–159: Design by Barbara Brock, A Proper Place, and Kathleen Ong, professional organizer, New York, New York. Shelving: Astech Closet Systems, 270 W. 36th St., NY, NY 10018; 212/244-6970 or 1/877-4-CLOZET; astechclosets.com. Brass expandable curtain rod with ceiling-mounted rod holders: The Home Depot. Brass clutch rings: The Home Depot and Bed Bath & Beyond

Laundry Rooms, Basements, Garages

Page 171: detergent unit: "Laundry Mate," Lillian Vernon Corp., One Theall Rd., Rye, NY, 10580; 800/901-9402

Page 174: chrome shelving: Hold Everything; 800/421-2264. Or visit holdeverything.com to view an online catalog, order a catalog, or find store locations

Page 181: laundry armoire, ROBIN wardrobe: IKEA Home Furnishings; 800/434-4532. Iron mounting board kits available at home centers

Page 183: Rubbermaid garage system, garden tower, and corner tool tower available at home improvement centers and organizing stores. For more information, visit rubbermaid.com

Pages 184–185: Elfa Garage Gardening Solution, Elfa Garage Sports Equipment Solution, Grook Tool Holder and Multi Store Rack available from The Container Store. Visit containerstore.com for store locations. Elfa Garage Sports Equipment Solution (about $356) and Garage Gardening Solution (about $390) require a minimum 6 feet in height and come with mounting hardware for drywall, wood, and masonry. The Container Store custom-designs units for small spaces at no charge.

Page 187: Hyloft USA-patented ceiling-mounted shelves can be hung at various levels depending on ceiling height. Units hold up to 250 pounds and provide up to 30 cubic feet storage space. Each unit sells for less than $90. Available at home improvement centers; visit hyloft.com

INDEX

INDEX